Making
The Music
Decision

Making The Music Decision

REVISED AND ENLARGED EDITION OF *FACING UP TO THE MUSIC*

JACK R. CHRISTIANSON

BOOKCRAFT
Salt Lake City, Utah

Library of Congress Catalog Card Number: 95-77390
ISBN 0-88494-990-7

First Printing, 1995

Printed in the United States of America

For Melanie

For my soul delighteth in the song of the heart; yea, the song of the righteous is a prayer unto me, and it shall be answered with a blessing upon their heads.

—Doctrine and Covenants 25:12

Music is part of the language of the Gods. It has been given to man so he can sing praises to the Lord. It is a means of expressing, with poetic words and in melodious tunes, the deep feelings of rejoicing and thanksgiving found in the hearts of those who have testimonies of the divine Sonship and who know of the wonders and glories wrought for them by the Father, Son, and Holy Spirit. Music is both in the voice and in the heart. . . .

Unfortunately not all music is good and edifying. Lucifer uses much that goes by the name of music to lead people to that which does not edify and is not of God. Just as language can be used to bless or curse, so music is a means of singing praises to the Lord or of planting evil thoughts and desires in the minds of men.

—Bruce R. McConkie

Contents

Acknowledgments

As always, this book could not have been published without the help of many. The extra mile efforts of several are particularly appreciated: thanks to MarLaine Layton and Kent Flowers for their help with the manuscript after several chapters were lost on the computer; a sincere gesture of gratitude to Kerry Stevenson and Kelly Johnson for their hours of computer assistance; sincere appreciation for Cory Maxwell and the staff at Bookcraft for allowing me to redo a project very close to my heart; and a special thanks and love for all the parents who have struggled with children who have made inappropriate decisions—they are the major inspiration behind this work.

This book is not an official publication of The Church of Jesus Christ of Latter-day Saints and is not endorsed by any of the Church leaders quoted within its pages. I alone am responsible for the ideas presented and accept complete responsibility for the work.

Music is one of the most forceful instruments for
governing the mind and spirit of man.
—William E. Gladstone

1

A Spiritual Approach to a Sensitive Subject

My love affair with music began when I was a young child. I loved listening to the radio and to my oldest sister's record player. She would play 45s and I would sing along with them by the hour.

I loved singing in elementary school programs. I remember getting chills up my arms and down my back as meaningful lyrics touched my heart and melodies entered my ears. I fantasized that someday I would perform in front of millions of people. Many afternoons after school found me at the home of my good friend Jon Mitchell, listening to Beatles records. We would stand on the hearth of his fireplace, he with his head next to one speaker and I with my head next to the other. We used old wooden tennis rackets as our imaginary guitars, and with the music blasting out of the speakers, we strummed the strings of the rackets and sang at the top of our lungs such classics as "Eight Days a Week" and "Nowhere Man."

It wasn't long before I finally received a real guitar for Christmas, and my dream of becoming a singing and performing star grew. I took organ lessons and played the trumpet in the junior high school band. Music was playing a major role in my young life. I loved it! I wanted to be involved in it constantly. Three or four of my classmates felt the same way. It didn't take long before we decided it was time to form our own band. "The Backstreets" were born in either Scott Shumway's garage or Gary Sabin's basement. We met. We planned. We dreamed.

We practiced until our parents nearly went crazy! We played songs from the Beatles, the Rolling Stones, the Animals, the Doors, Cream, and many, many other bands. (I didn't understand then—but I do now—why some of my behaviors and attitudes were the way they were. I was totally influenced by the music I listened to and performed.) Along with every other band during that time period we played "Wipe Out," "Hey Joe," and "Louie Louie." We hustled jobs just about anywhere we could get them. We played at a local restaurant and at junior high and high school dances. We even played at a couple of college dances. We felt that we were getting pretty good.

With great excitement we practiced and prepared the classic Jim Morrison song "Light My Fire" for the big assembly at school. When the time arrived to perform, there was no turning back. We were terrified to perform in front of all our peers. However, it was now or never. We had to perform; if for no other reason, we had purchased matching outfits of blue blazers, white turtlenecks, white pants, and black shoes. We couldn't let our parents' money go to waste.

We did it! It was more than fun, it was exhilarating. Some students even liked it! In fact, we were asked to perform again in front of the entire student body.

From there we entered several "Battle of the Bands" contests throughout the state. We didn't win any first place trophies, but we did well. However, a band from our high school won the national Battle of the Bands contest, which gave us the motivation to keep trying, even when some of the neighbors called the police on us for making so much noise in my mom and dad's carport.

As the years passed and each of our lives changed, so did

our interests. I developed a great love for sports and wanted to pursue a career as an athlete. In order to do so, my music had to be set aside for a few years. Those few years turned into many, and my deep interest in music was not rekindled until I found myself teaching English and coaching in a high school north of Salt Lake City. My students seemed to have such keen interest in music that I decided to use it as a tool in the teaching process. Poetry units came alive for most students when they realized that some of the modern musicians were actually poets. Many names of the artists were familiar to the students, and studying poetry began to be much more palatable. While teaching about Walt Whitman, Robert Frost, and Emily Dickinson, we wove in the works of Paul McCartney, Paul Simon, and Jim Morrison. Most students became very excited to study and begin writing their own poetry.

When I was hired to teach seminary for the Church Educational System, I found, as you will read in the following chapters, that music plays a vital role in almost all areas of our lives. After having several challenging encounters with students and their feelings about music, I began an intense research project on the influences of music on our actions, feelings, thoughts, and spirituality. With the help of many students and several music professionals my office was soon filled with numerous records, tapes, videos, news articles, magazine clippings, research papers, and books, all on the subject of popular music as well as music in general.

After giving a lesson in class and speaking at several firesides on the topic, I sensed something big was about to happen. Many people accepted what was being said about music and its influences, but there were many who were downright angry. I felt somewhat like Joseph Smith may have felt when the angel Moroni told him that his name "should be both good and evil spoken of among all people" (Joseph Smith—History 1:33).

I never dreamed that music was such a sensitive issue with so many people and that it could elicit such a wide range of emotional responses. I learned that it was not just a sensitive issue with the youth. Some of the greatest opposition came from adults who didn't want to give up that which they had treasured for so long.

I remember being discouraged and not wanting to write or speak about the influences of music anymore. All the opposition I was experiencing from the adversary did not appear to be worth it. I wanted to quit. In fact, I even left the teaching profession for a while because I felt that it wasn't worth it anymore. Then I started to think about the words of a song by the heavy metal band AC\DC. As I thought of the words, I almost got angry. OK, I did get angry. I had only heard the song a few times, but I had at one time read the lyrics in my lectures to make a point. However, I never felt comfortable giving Satan time in an LDS meeting. In fact, sometimes it's very easy to encourage the very thing we are trying to prevent by talking about it too much or in too much detail, or by exposing the audience to that which is not of God. So I eliminated the song from my presentation. The song is titled "Hell's Bells," and the lead singer screams out in a high, grating voice, "Nobody's putting up a fight. I got my bell, I'm gonna take you to hell, I'm gonna get ya, Satan's gonna get ya, Hell's Bells."

I could almost picture Satan laughing as the words "nobody's putting up a fight" ran through my mind. Those words were just not true! I would put up a fight! The Apostles and prophets of God were putting up a fight! That song was a lie! There were many Latter-day Saints as well as non-Latter-day Saints who would fight. Just because some people would get angry and others would mock, was that any reason to stop trying to help young people and their parents learn to choose appropriate music? Of course not!

It was necessary to do what I could in this area without it becoming a personal hobbyhorse. I believe I have done that. For this reason I have decided to try one more time to write about music. My desire is to help those who are willing to listen to make wise, educated decisions concerning the music they choose to listen to or the music videos they choose to watch.

As each reader makes these decisions, he or she should not forget the timely words of Elder James E. Faust. While speaking at a BYU devotional Elder Faust quoted the words of Elder Marion G. Romney concerning the principle that you cannot teach the true gospel of Jesus Christ without offending Satan. He said:

> I owe my text to Elder Marion G. Romney who, at a BYU Devotional in 1955, stated: "Now there are those among us who are trying to serve the Lord without offending the devil." This is a contradiction of terms. President Romney goes on: "Must the choice lie irrevocably between peace on the one hand, obtained by compliance with the gospel of Jesus Christ as restored through the Prophet Joseph Smith, and contention and war on the other hand?" . . .
>
> President Romney continues: "The consequences of [mortal man's] choices are of the all-or-nothing sort. There is no way for him to escape the influence of these opposing powers. Inevitably he is led by one or the other. His God-given free agency gives him the power and option to choose. But choose he must. Nor can he serve both of them at the same time, for, as Jesus said, 'No man can serve two masters: . . . Ye cannot serve God and mammon.'"
>
> . . . I think we will witness increasing evidence of Satan's power as the kingdom of God grows stronger. I believe Satan's ever-expanding efforts are some proof of the truthfulness of this work. In the future the opposition will be both more subtle and more open. It will be masked in greater sophistication and cunning, but it will also be more blatant. We will need greater spirituality to perceive all of the forms of evil and greater strength to resist it.[1]

Nephi taught a similar lesson in these words:

> And now it came to pass that after I, Nephi, had made an end of speaking to my brethren, behold they said unto me: Thou hast declared unto us hard things, more than we are able to bear.

> And it came to pass that I said unto them that I knew that I had spoken hard things against the wicked, according to the truth; and the righteous have I justified, and testified that they should be lifted up at the last day; wherefore, the guilty taketh the truth to be hard, for it cutteth them to the very center. (1 Nephi 16:1–2.)

The truth about any subject, not just music and music videos, is not an easy taskmaster. Truth requires us to look at the issues as they really are and as they really will be (see Jacob 4:13), not just as they may appear on the surface. Truth, if we do not fear it, may cause us to change our opinions, admit that we may have been wrong in the past, or accept something that previously rubbed us the wrong way. As the classic Mormon film *Man's Search for Happiness* states, "Only if you are unafraid of truth will you ever find it."[2] This concept of never fearing truth will be covered further in chapter 8 of this book.

As we begin this reading adventure together concerning this most sensitive topic, please lower any walls of defense and pray for the guidance of the Holy Spirit. Please remember that I in no way claim to be an authority in the field of music. However, I am also not just some geeky religion teacher who thinks he is "Roger Rocker" and is going to say that you are not going to make it into the celestial kingdom if you listen to inappropriate music. I am a teacher and author who loves young people with all my heart. Much has been learned since my music days in the '60s. I desire to help educate so that perhaps "there might not be more sorrow upon all the face of the earth" (Alma 29:2).

President Spencer W. Kimball, while speaking in 1976 at the Sydney Australia Area Conference concerning the law of chastity, taught a valuable lesson concerning true principles and personal opinions. He said:

> I do not hesitate to bring this matter to your attention, for I know that this is not a matter of personal opinion. A young

man who was seated near me at my office sought to argue with me on this. He said, "Now, but Brother Kimball, I respect your opinion, but that's *your* opinion. And this is my opinion."

He was a young man with limited experience and he thought his opinion was as good as mine. I hastily rejoined, "Yes, my dear boy. If what you say is true, if this is just a matter of opinions—yours against mine, I might back off, admitting that with your intelligence and careful thinking, perhaps your opinion might be even much better than mine, and I would yield. But here is a great disparity. It is your opinion against mine bolstered and strengthened by the combined inspiration and revelation of the ages.

"There were the inspiration and revelation of Adam and of Seth and Enoch. There were the combined revelations of Noah and Shem and Abraham and Moses. There were added revelations of Joshua and Solomon, Isaiah, and Jeremiah. We have also the Lord's revelations to numerous other of the great spiritual leaders, including Peter, James, John, and Paul and even the Lord Jesus Christ himself, and all of the modern prophets alike including Joseph, and Brigham, and John, and Wilford, and Lorenzo, and Heber—all have known that these things are sins and transgressions, so I add my little voice to say it again. I do not fear to tell you that your little opinion is most insignificant alongside all these. We know whereof we speak. These are rank sins and unholy transgressions. And I call on you to accept this."[3]

The purpose of this book is not to give the reader my personal opinions on what music I feel is or is not appropriate. I wish only to share what the scriptures teach and what some of the prophets have said on the subject. If it were just my opinion, then I, like President Kimball, would back down and let the issue die without writing another word. However, it is "mine bolstered and strengthened by the combined inspiration and revelation of the ages." The following chapters present a spiritual approach to this sensitive subject. Each prophet of this dispensation has added his voice to the voices mentioned by

President Kimball in the preceding quotation. The fact of the matter is, if we could simply learn to "listen to a prophet's voice," this book would not be necessary. The prophets have spoken. In the *For the Strength of Youth* pamphlet the First Presidency covered the issue in three brief paragraphs. They wrote:

> Our Heavenly Father has counseled us as Latter-day Saints to seek after "anything virtuous, lovely, or of good report or praiseworthy" (Articles of Faith 1:13). Whatever you read, listen to, or watch makes an impression on you. Public entertainment and the media can provide you with much positive experience. They can uplift and inspire you, teach you good and moral principles, and bring you closer to the beauty this world offers. But they can also make what is wrong and evil look normal, exciting, and acceptable. . . .
>
> Music can help you draw closer to your Heavenly Father. It can be used to educate, edify, inspire, and unite. However, music may be used for wicked purposes. Music can, by its tempo, beat, intensity, and lyrics, dull your spiritual sensitivity. You cannot afford to fill your minds with unworthy music. Music is an important and powerful part of life. You must consider your listening habits thoughtfully and prayerfully. You should be willing to control your listening habits and shun music that is spiritually harmful. Don't listen to music that contains ideas that contradict principles of the gospel. Don't listen to music that promotes Satanism or other evil practices, encourages immorality, uses foul and offensive language, or drives away the Spirit. Use careful judgment and maturity to choose the music you listen to and the level of its volume.[4]

Music truly is the language of the gods and the devils. Both use it to promote their work and to build their kingdoms. One of our great challenges is to choose only that music and other entertainment that brings lasting happiness and glorifies our Father in Heaven. My hope is that this book may help you in some small way to do so.

*Make wholesome music of all kinds
a part of your life.
—Boyd K. Packer*

2

Music and
Our Lives

How important is music in your life? If you're like most people you would find it difficult to live without music in some form or another on a regular basis. Very few lives are not affected profoundly by this magnificent means of communication. Regardless of what we choose to listen to—whether it be rock, jazz, classical, country western, new wave, punk, heavy metal, reggae, rap, grunge, alternative, speed metal, death rock, devotional, religious, or elevator music—in most instances the music has a noticeable effect on our actions, feelings, thoughts, and spirituality, not to mention many hair and clothing styles. Simply put, we are seriously influenced by our musical and visual diet. I believe we are as much what we listen to and watch as we are what we eat. We become what we think about most of the time (see Proverbs 23:7). Whatever we choose to fill our minds with influences our behavior. Actions, feelings, and attitudes all grow out of our thought patterns.

Volumes have been written about music. Armies have been motivated by it; teenagers camp for days to purchase tickets to hear it; athletic events would often be dull without it; movies and television have come alive because of it; airwaves buzz with it; prophets, as well as their followers, sing praises to God through it; and unfortunately many families have been and are becoming divided or disrupted by it.

I know of few things that can influence human behavior more than the powers of music. It is one of the most powerful stimuli known. Like food, music can be enjoyed immensely without a knowledge of how it was prepared or packaged. Perhaps this is why so many people, young and old alike, are involved so deeply and so often in their music. It is a chance to fantasize, to live dreams through the successes and lives of others in the private and sometimes quiet chambers of our minds. By immersing ourselves in music, it is possible to escape the many pressures and stressful situations created by our modern society.

Music has been one of the most common expressions of man's feelings since the beginning of human history. Man has always sung. Many of the great thinkers of antiquity emphasized the powerful effect of music upon the character of man. Confucius, Plato, Aristotle, and many, many others were convinced that music molded character. Perhaps the old axiom "As in music, so in life" is more of a truism than we have realized.

For civilized man, music has become an international language. Feelings can be communicated by music that words simply cannot express. Though the words may be in different languages, the music communicates to the soul. President David O. McKay illustrated this idea when he said:

> We do not have any thoughts that cannot be expressed either in words or gestures, but there are feelings in the human heart which cannot be expressed in any language or words; so we must provide ourselves with other mediums of expression; for instance, music, art, architecture—the wonderful arts which do not belong to any nation, but which speak the language of the soul. Music is international. Although the words may be Polynesian or Italian or German or English, music is always understood by the soul.

Music is a divine art. And the people who love music are not a bad people. But there is in music that which appeals also to the baser emotions of man; but the music of which we speak lifts us up and brings us to a nobler and better sphere, and I am glad that I belong to a church that from the beginning has held this divine art as an ideal.[1]

More recently the First Presidency of The Church of Jesus Christ of Latter-day Saints has said: "Through music, man's ability to express himself extends beyond the limits of the spoken language in both subtlety and power. Music can be used to exalt and inspire or to carry messages of degradation and destruction. It is therefore important that as Latter-day Saints we at all times apply the principles of the gospel and seek the guidance of the Spirit in selecting the music with which we surround ourselves."[2]

If we do not fear the truth and honestly approach the study of the influences of music in our lives, it is just about impossible to say that music does not affect us in one way or another. Surveys have shown that the average American teenager listens to more than four hours of music each day.[3] If this survey continues to be even remotely accurate, then there are very few teenagers anywhere in the modern world who are not influenced and who do not hear a number of hours of music each day.

Sometime ago while hunting deer with my father in the mountains of central Utah, I had an experience that helped me better understand the pervasive and all-encompassing nature of music. We hiked to the top of a rather high knoll. When we reached our predetermined destination, we found a comfortable hiding spot under a tall, bushy pine tree and awaited the arrival of our winter dinner. A beautiful sight opened to our view as we sat and watched the mountain below us as well as the vast mountain range surrounding our secluded perch. There were miles and miles of tree-covered hills on all sides of us, with meadows of sagebrush and tall grass spotting each ravine and gully.

There I sat, alone with my dad, exchanging whispered conversation, drinking ice-cold water from a canteen, and eating apples and miniature Hershey chocolate bars. It was wonderful! It was the first time we had hunted together for several years, and neither of us was too interested in killing a deer. We simply wanted to be together and enjoy the beauty and wonder of being in the mountains and away from the pressures of the valley.

As the sun fought to make its way over a group of early morning clouds, we enjoyed each other's company and the bliss of that moment. Then, without warning, the bliss was interrupted as the soft eastern wind brought with it, of all things, the sound of an electric guitar. It became louder and louder with each second. It wasn't long before we spied the source of the piercing rhythms bouncing their way up the mountainside. A would-be hunter in a fairly late model four-wheel drive pickup, evidently with an outrageous sound system, was enjoying his music at an extremely high volume level. When he reached the top of the knoll below us he stopped the truck, opened the door, and stepped out. I could not believe it! The speakers attached to the door were sending screams of music across the valleys and dells, with little respect for the two hunters sitting beneath a pine tree. If there had been deer in the immediate area, they were now well on their way to a new and more quiet hiding place.

When the guy finally turned off his stereo system, I turned to my dad and said, "See, Dad, what have I been telling you? Music is everywhere! We can't even get away from it in the tops of the mountains."

Without saying a word, he raised his rifle to his shoulder and clicked a shell into the chamber. I sat watching as he aimed his rifle at the cab of the truck. "Well, I can get away from it, son," he said, chuckling under his breath.

"No, Dad!" I laughed, reaching for the barrel of his gun. He ejected the shell out of the chamber, looked at me, and we both started to laugh. "I guess you're right, son. I guess some people just can't live without it, can they?"

Obviously we didn't get a deer, but we both learned something about music. We learned that just about everywhere we go, even to the tops of the mountains, music is all around us.

Think about it. Could you go thirty consecutive days without listening to any type of music whatsoever? Even thinking of it is difficult. Some readers may even go through withdrawals while considering the idea. I invite anyone to try it. You will find it is almost impossible. Why? Because music is everywhere! Thirty days with no music means no shopping at the local supermarket. No visits to the dentist's or doctor's office. No shopping at the mall! You can't even get put on hold on the telephone if you don't want to hear music. No music for thirty days means no live athletic events, no television, no videos or movies, no radio, no concerts, no dances, no parades, no plays, not much of anything. In fact, we wouldn't even be able to attend most schools. It is difficult to walk down the hall of any public high school without hearing a myriad of different types of music. Thirty days with no music would also mean we would not be able to attend church meetings either. In Doctrine and Covenants 25:12 the Lord tells Emma Smith, "For my soul delighteth in the song of the heart; yea, the song of the righteous is a prayer unto me, and it shall be answered with a blessing upon their heads." If the songs of the heart or the songs of the righteous are prayers unto the Lord, then we can hardly expect those who worship God not to pray to him in song.

Two other questions must be asked when considering the songs of the heart and the songs of the righteous as prayers unto God. First, if the songs of the righteous are prayers unto God, what are the songs of the unrighteous? Are they prayers to someone else? And second, if the songs of our hearts are prayers to God, which God do some of us pray to? I know for me it is difficult to not sing the last two or three lines of the last song I heard on the radio all day long! These words seem to run through my mind continually. What if the words are promoting immoral sexual behavior, drug or alcohol abuse, parental hatred, suicide, witchcraft, devil worship or the occult, or any principle contrary to the teachings of Christ? Can we honestly say we are praying to the god we know as our Father in Heaven? It sure is something to consider.

Thirty days without music would be practically impossible. Oh, it might be done with a great deal of work and effort, but for most it would be a very difficult task. After all, what is the first thing many people do when they get up in the morning, especially teenagers? Don't they turn on the radio or CD player? Some even wake up to a clock radio! The first thing pumped into their systems every day of their lives is music. How can we say that it will not have a profound effect on our actions, feelings, thoughts, and spirit?

Not only is it the first thing we often do in the morning, but many times it is also one of the first things we do when we get into a car of any kind. After starting the engine we almost immediately begin to push buttons and turn knobs until we find the tune we want, and then a strange human phenomenon occurs. The windows go up, and we begin to have our own concert inside the car. The person driving begins to tap out the rhythm of the tune on the steering wheel. Sometimes he even sings into his thumb, using it as an imaginary microphone. The person in the passenger seat plays his imaginary drums or piano on the dashboard. Heads begin to bob like large birds during a courting ritual, and facial expressions, along with sincere and serious singing, tell the story of the music being listened to. Some people speed up or slow down or just kind of space out, depending on the kind of music they are digesting.

It is hilarious to pull up beside people like this and watch as they fantasize themselves into the dream world of being a star. Most of the time these stoplight performers have no idea how they are acting until they look over at someone in another car who is watching and being entertained. They immediately realize they are making fools of themselves and flip their heads forward in embarrassment and conclude their concert. However, when some people know they have an audience they intensify their level of performance, to the enjoyment of all who are watching.

If listening to music is the first thing many people do when they get up in the morning and one of the first things they do when they get into a car, what is the last thing many people do before they go to bed at night? Some people can't even sleep without the narcotic of music. Yet some claim it has no effect on them. How many parents or brothers or sisters have crept silently into a loved one's room late at night or early in the morning to turn off a radio or CD player that was left on because the room's occupant was unable to sleep without it playing?

With this type of powerful influence in our lives, would it not be wise to be cautious when choosing the type of music we listen to? It is important and can be a wonderful, exhilarating form of entertainment. However, if misused it can become a very degrading or demoralizing activity.

There is little argument that youth entertainment is a lucrative part of the leisure activity market. Some studies have shown that teenagers listen to an estimated 10,500 hours of rock music between the seventh and the twelfth grades. That works out to just about five hundred fewer hours than the time they spend in school for twelve years. Children between the ages of two and twelve watch an average of twenty-five hours of television a week, most of that television being accompanied by musical score.[4]

Contention in a home is one of the great tragedies of life. Ofttimes music can be a contributing factor to that contention. When someone yells down the hall, "Turn that garbage down!" what is the most common reaction of the person being yelled at? Isn't it usually to turn the music up instead? Battle lines are drawn over what is acceptable and what is not. Parents at times become enraged with some of the popular music, and children sometimes feel that their parents' music is old-fashioned and slow. It becomes a contest of wills. Each defends his position of who is right and who is wrong rather than what is right.

With the rising of tempers it is soon forgotten that just because a person likes the music does not make it appropriate, and just because he or she dislikes it does not make it inappropriate. For this reason we must base our decisions concerning music on true principles rather than on personal likes and dislikes. For example, we may enjoy the feeling of driving a car off a three-hundred-foot cliff. It's probably a real rush all the way to the bottom. However, when the car hits the ground we're talking major-duty pain. Just because you may enjoy the ride does not mean it's good. So it is with music. Just because you enjoy what you are listening to does not mean it is appropriate or acceptable, because it may negatively affect your actions, feelings, thoughts, or spirituality. In the same vein, just because an adult may enjoy easy-listening music does not mean it is totally appropriate. If the music is "acceptable" but the lyrics promote adultery, can it not help but have a negative effect on one's behaviors or feelings? On the other hand, just because you dislike a particular genre of music does not mean it's inappropriate. Again, personal likes and dislikes are not valid criteria for choosing appropriate music.

Concerning this issue of personal opinion verses true principles, President Spencer W. Kimball taught,

> This true way of life [the gospel] is not a matter of opinion. There are absolute truths and relative truths. . . . There are many ideas advanced to the world that have been changed to meet the needs of the truth as it has been discovered. There are relative truths, and there are also absolute truths which are the same yesterday, today, and forever—never changing. These absolute truths are not altered by the opinions of men. . . .
>
> . . . In short, opinion alone has no power in the matter of an absolute truth.[5]

When it comes to music we must follow the true principles laid down by the Lord in the scriptures and by living Apostles and prophets, rather than having contention over what we like or dislike. We must never forget that contention in any form is not of God. In fact, the Savior taught the Nephites in 3 Nephi 11:29–30 that "he that hath the spirit of contention is not of me, but is of the devil, who is the father of contention, and he stirreth up the hearts of men to contend with anger, one with another. Behold, this is not my doctrine, to stir up the hearts of men with anger, one against another; but this is my doctrine, that such things should be done away." Part of the doctrine of Christ is to do away with contention, not to stir it up.

Is there contention in your home over music? If there is, hopefully the following stories will aid you in understanding the power music can have when used as a tool to dispel contention, and at times to create it if wisdom is not used. Wisdom becomes vital when families are in disagreement concerning this sensitive subject. Some good advice is the same as that which the prophet Jacob, the brother of Nephi, gave: "O be wise; what can I say more?" (Jacob 6:12.)

Contention, like so many other things, is a tool of the adversary to destroy individuals and families. For me, there is no worse feeling than to be at odds with those I love most. A feeling of darkness prevails, and a sickening nausea and emptiness converges upon me. On the other hand, there is perhaps no greater feeling than to have harmony and peace with my loved ones.

I remember a time in my youth when I had a disagreement with my mother. I cried, complained, and even threatened to run away. It was an idle threat, but I threatened to do it nevertheless. After a few minutes of disagreement I could stand it no longer. I headed for my bedroom with the intention of slamming the door, getting my jacket, and leaving for good.

As I hurried down the hallway I cried out, "You don't love me anymore! You never let me do anything!" The funny thing is, I don't even remember why we were having the disagreement.

When my mother heard that I thought she didn't love me, she said something that caused chills to run through my body.

She commanded, "Young man, you stop right there!" Please trust me—when my mother said stop, you had better stop! I knew she meant business. She was the type who wouldn't hesitate to chase me down the block, tackle me on the neighbors' lawn, and then bring me home by any means necessary. Seldom, if ever, did she wait for my father to return home before taking care of the problem herself.

I stopped and, with a quivering voice, cried again, "Why should I? You don't love me anymore. You never let me do anything!"

After telling me to stop a second time, she brushed by me and went into her bedroom. She returned shortly with a suitcase in her hands. I stood and watched in utter amazement as she entered my bedroom, pulled out the dresser drawers, and filled the suitcase with many of my clothes. After snapping the suitcase shut, our eyes met. I could see her true sweetness but tried to ignore it. I knew she could sense that I was uncomfortable and did not know how to handle such an abrupt action— I mean, after all, I was her sweet, spoiled baby boy. I had always felt that she thought I was something special. But now I didn't know what to think, and she knew it!

We were still exchanging bold stares when she spoke and nearly broke my heart. "Jackie," she said, handing me the suitcase, "if you think you can find a better mother than me, or one who loves you more than me, go ahead, leave."

My little broken heart was telling me not to leave, but my pride told me I needed to teach her a lesson (ha ha ha). I left.

Where was I to go? In the early 1960s in Orem, Utah, the only alternatives were the playgrounds at the school; the apple, peach, pear, or cherry orchards surrounding our home; the irrigation ditch; or the horse trailer parked in the field behind our house. The horse trailer won out. I climbed on the outside wheel well, threw my suitcase in, and climbed in after it.

I remember how terrible it was to be in the trailer. It obviously hadn't been cleaned in years. It was filthy, and the smell was almost stifling. However, I was determined to stay there no matter what and, as I said, teach my parents a big lesson.

It wasn't long before I fell asleep. I didn't wake up until I heard my dog barking and jumping up and down at the side of the trailer. When I came to my senses, I could hear my dad calling my name. I quickly tried to quiet the dog before he gave my hiding place away. However, it was too late. In the middle of one of my quieting attempts, the trailer tipped to one side—the moment of reckoning had come! My dad had climbed up on the wheel well and was peering down at me like death itself.

Up until that time in my life I wasn't sure if the Lord really answered prayers, but I'll tell you, I prayed without ceasing for deliverance. Almost before my prayers had a chance to get out of the trailer, my dad commanded in his deep and somewhat angry voice, "Young man, get out of the trailer now!" I was petrified, so I pretended I was asleep. He gave the command once more. I continued to pretend. He didn't wait to ask a third time. With one motion he reached down with his thick hand and pulled me over the side of the trailer and set me on my feet. My hands immediately went to my backside for protection. However, the expected swat never came. Instead, he placed his strong but loving arm around my shoulders and said, "Oh, son, I'm so glad I found you. Your mother and I have been worried sick. Won't you come home and eat dinner with us?"

I replied with a sigh of relief and thanksgiving, "Uh . . . yeah, I guess I could."

We walked arm in arm back to the house. As we walked through the door and down the hallway, I could smell the familiar aroma of my mother's cooking. When I reached the end of the hallway, I stood at the bottom of the two steps that led into the kitchen. There she stood, her apron smudged with spills, her hair disheveled, her glasses on the end of her nose, and tears in her eyes. She walked to where I was standing, knelt down on the floor, and placed her tender hands on my cheeks. This time, as she looked in my eyes, I melted and my pride ran back to the horse trailer. She cried and said softly, "Oh, Jackie, will you ever forgive me for being such a terrible mother?"

I fell into her arms and muttered through my tears, "You're the best mother in the whole world!"

As I look back in time and compare the nausea of fighting with the bliss of harmony, my heart aches. Why are we so foolish as to let little insignificant items destroy the beauty of peaceful homes? Why are some young people and their parents willing to let the most sacred and important relationships in their lives—those with their families—be marred or damaged for such minor, temporary things as the cost of a CD that will only be popular for a short time or a video or concert ticket? Music does play an important role in controlling or contributing to contentious situations in our daily lives, as well as in our homes.

Elder Gene R. Cook of the First Quorum of the Seventy had a startling experience while riding on a plane with Mick Jagger, the lead singer for the Rolling Stones. They discussed many items of importance, including contention over music within the family unit. Elder Cook later said about this experience:

> He told me the importance, in his view, of freeing up the youth. He felt that they ought to be able to do whatever they wanted in spite of their parents. He said that parents were inhibiting them too much and controlling things and they ought not be doing that. It was truly astounding to me. He told me he was thankful the family, as an entity, was being destroyed. And I gathered from what he was saying that he was doing his best to help that along.[6]

This supports statements made earlier by Mr. Jagger in an article which appeared in *Newsweek* magazine in 1982. He said, "There's no future in rock 'n' roll. It's only recycled past. . . . Basically, rock 'n' roll isn't protest, and never was. It's only—it promotes interfamilial tension. It used to. Now it can't even do that, because fathers don't ever get outraged with the music. Either they like it, or it sounds similar to what they liked as kids. So rock 'n' roll's gone, that's all gone."[7] Perhaps this is why some artists have moved into areas in their performing that will offend many parents.

What are we to believe when at least one well-known performer is so vocal about the fact that much of his music is written for the specific purpose of causing contention in families? It's frightening. In fact, the lead singer of one group declared . that he and the other group members "wanted to be the group parents hate." Why? Because then music would be purchased as an act of rebellion, thus increasing the performers' financial security. Money is the name of the game for music promoters. Little thought is given to the effects on the consumer. If a product generates revenue, it is produced.

Contrast these attitudes with those of President Heber J. Grant. He described the beautiful power of music and how it can soothe irritated feelings and a contentious spirit.

> I recall one incident showing how song has the power to soothe irritated feelings and bring harmony to the hearts of men who are filled with a contentious spirit. It occurred many years ago, and involved a quarrel between two old and faithful brethren whose membership dated back to the days of Nauvoo. They had been through many of the hardships of Nauvoo, and had suffered the drivings and persecutions of the Saints, as well as the hardships of pioneering incident to the early settlement of the West. These men had quarreled over some business affairs, and finally concluded that they would try to get President John Taylor to help them adjust their difficulties.
>
> John Taylor was then the president of the Council of the Twelve Apostles. These brethren pledged their word of honor that they would faithfully abide by whatever decision Brother Taylor might render. Like many others, even in these days, they were not willing to accept the conclusions and counsels of their teachers, or bishops, or presidents of stakes, who would have been the authorized persons, in their order, to consult, and which would have been the proper course to pursue, but they must have some higher authority. Having been personally acquainted with President Brigham Young, in the days of Nauvoo, and feeling their importance in their own devotion to the work of the Lord, nothing short of an Apostle's advice would seem to satisfy them.

Accordingly they called on President Taylor, but did not immediately tell him what their trouble was, but explained that they had seriously quarreled and asked him if he would listen to their story and render his decision. President Taylor willingly consented. But he said: "Brethren, before I hear your case, I would like very much to sing one of the songs of Zion for you." Now President Taylor was a very capable singer, and interpreted sweetly and with spirit, our sacred hymns. He sang one of our hymns to the two brethren. Seeing its effect, he remarked that he never heard one of the songs of Zion but that he wanted to listen to one more, and so asked them to listen while he sang another. Of course, they consented. They both seemed to enjoy it; and, having sung the second song, he remarked that he had heard there is luck in odd numbers and so with their consent he would sing still another, which he did. Then, in his jocular way, he remarked: "Now brethren, I do not want to wear you out, but if you will forgive me, and listen to one more hymn, I promise to stop singing, and will hear your case."

The story goes that when President Taylor had finished the fourth song, the brethren were melted to tears, got up, shook hands, and asked President Taylor to excuse them for having called upon him, and for taking up his time. They then departed without his even knowing what their difficulties were.

President Taylor's singing had reconciled their feelings toward each other. The Spirit of the Lord had entered their hearts, and the hills of difference that rose between them had been leveled and become as nothing. Love and brotherhood had developed in their souls, and the trifles over which they had quarreled, had become of no consequence in their sight. The songs of the heart had filled them with the spirit of reconciliation.[8]

In my own home, when our children were younger, my wife and I used to try to dispel the irritating and contentious feelings that can arise while putting children to bed at night by playing beautiful, inspiring music as they fell asleep. The results were amazing. What used to be a major battle zone became a pleasant experience most of the time.

After playing the music for several nights, the children would ask for music to fall asleep to nearly every night. It seemed to have a calming influence on them as well as to dispel their fears. They were seldom afraid of the dark because the music filled their minds with beautiful thoughts and inspiring words.

Oh, that we could only let the beautiful powers of music fill our minds and souls. Music is important in our lives, much more so than most of us have realized. William E. Gladstone, a nineteenth century British prime minister, put it this way: "Music is one of the most forceful instruments for governing the mind and spirit of man."[9]

Hopefully each of us will be more conscious of the magnificent power of music—and also of some of its destructive powers—so that we may enjoy appropriate music as one of God's greatest creations. And hopefully music will become to us as it was to Henry Wadsworth Longfellow when he expressed in his poem "Christus": "Yet music is the prophet's art. Among one of the gifts that God has sent, one of the most magnificent."

3

"For My Soul Delighteth in the Song of the Heart"

How important is the role of music in the process of receiving revelation from our Heavenly Father? The following story helps to answer this critical question.

The life of ten-year-old Bobby Jenkins seemed to be filled with turmoil. His parents were divorced and his father remarried a fine woman—but she just didn't seem to take the place of his real mother. To make matters worse, his oldest brother joined the Army.

This left him at home with his fifteen-year-old brother, Tim. He was the one person Bobby could rely on. They had been through so much together. Even though Tim was five years older, they were as close as brothers could be.

Then one day Bobby received news which caused the bottom of his world to drop out. Tim had drowned in a senseless accident while swimming in the canal.

During the funeral, Bobby seemed to go numb. He had been hurt so many times, he didn't want to feel again.

Except for school and other necessary activities, he hibernated in his room. He turned on the radio to the hardest rock music he could find. Hour after hour, day after day—even while he slept, the music blared. With its loud and constant rhythm, he didn't have to think or feel. He could separate himself from the world which had hurt him so deeply.

After many weeks of this, his stepmother couldn't stand it any longer. In the middle of the night, while Bobby was sleeping, she tiptoed into his room and turned off the radio.

The next morning he poked his head into the kitchen and asked, "Did you turn off my radio last night?"

Expecting the worst, his stepmother gently replied, "Yes, I did."

She didn't get the answer she had expected. Instead Bobby sat down at the table and softly shared the feelings of his heart.

"This morning when I woke up, Timmy appeared in my room. He told me he was happy and all was well. He said the Church is true and I should start reading the Book of Mormon. He told me lots of things which really made me happy."

Bobby stopped just long enough to gain his composure, then continued. "He said this was the fourth time he had received permission to visit me, but he couldn't come into my room because of the type of music I had on the radio."

With a hint of emotion in his voice, this ten-year-old man said, "Thanks, Mom, for turning off my radio."[1]

This true story may seem a bit dramatic until you stop to consider the doctrine taught by the Prophet Joseph Smith and by President Joseph F. Smith. Joseph Smith taught, "There are no angels who minister to this earth but those who do belong or have belonged to it." Commenting on this statement, President Joseph F. Smith said:

Hence, when messengers are sent to minister to the inhabitants of this earth, they are not strangers, but from the ranks of our kindred, friends, and fellow-beings and fellow-servants. . . . In like manner our fathers and mothers, brothers, sisters and friends who have passed away from this earth, having been faithful, and worthy to enjoy these rights and privileges, may have a mission given them to visit their relatives and friends upon the earth again, bringing from the divine Presence messages of love, of warning, or reproof and instruction, to those whom they had learned to love in the flesh.[2]

How often has the Lord tried to communicate with us? Not necessarily through angelic ministers, but to our hearts and our minds through the still small voice of the Spirit? How often have we not been able to receive it? When it comes to music, the entire issue, as far as I am concerned, is the matter of being able to receive or not to receive personal revelation. One of the objectives of this book is to help each individual understand the role of music in receiving revelation from our Father in Heaven through the Holy Ghost. The Lord says in the Doctrine and Covenants, "Yea, behold, I will tell you in your mind and in your heart, by the Holy Ghost, which shall come upon you and which shall dwell in your heart. Now, behold, this is the spirit of revelation." (D&C 8:2–3.)

If the Lord communicates to our minds and hearts by the power of the Holy Ghost, and the Holy Ghost whispers by a still small voice (see 1 Kings 19:12), how can we feel or hear the Spirit if we have filled our minds and hearts with irreverent music or images? Again, the issue of listening to appropriate or inappropriate music has nothing to do with adults trying to decide for young people what they can or cannot listen to, but it is to help them in their abilities to receive revelation.

Elder Boyd K. Packer taught us concerning this sacred subject. He said:

> This trend to more noise, more excitement, more contention, less restraint, less dignity, less formality is not coincidental nor innocent nor harmless.
>
> The first order issued by a commander mounting a military invasion is the jamming of the channels of communication of those he intends to conquer.

Irreverence suits the purposes of the adversary by obstructing the delicate channels of revelation in both mind and spirit.[3]

How often has the Lord tried to communicate with us but was unable to do so because we had static in our receiving system? How often has our music or videos been the source of that static? On the other hand, how often has the Lord communicated to us through music? Elder Bruce R. McConkie made a profound statement concerning these questions when he said, "Music is part of the language of the Gods. It has been given to man so he can sing praises to the Lord. It is a means of expressing, with poetic words and in melodious tunes, the deep feelings of rejoicing and thanksgiving found in the hearts of those who have testimonies of the divine Sonship and who know of the wonders and glories wrought for them by the Father, Son, and Holy Spirit. Music is both in the voice and in the heart."[4]

How important is music to the Lord? In chapter 2 we discussed Doctrine and Covenants 25:12, which states that the Lord delights in the song of the heart and that the song of the righteous is a prayer unto him, "and it shall be answered with a blessing upon their heads." The book of Psalms in the Old Testament contains hymns that were sung in the temple.

We read that on the night Jesus was born his birth was announced by angels singing, "And suddenly there was with the angel a multitude of the heavenly host praising God, and saying, Glory to God in the highest, and on earth peace, good will toward men" (Luke 2:13–14).

One of the last things Jesus did on this earth before going into the Garden of Gethsemane to atone for all mankind—the single greatest event in the history of the universe—was to sing a song with his Apostles. Mark 14:26 reads, "And when they had sung an hymn, they went out into the mount of Olives." Did Jesus understand the power of music to help himself prepare for the great ordeal that awaited him? And did he also understand the strength the Apostles might need as they embarked on an uncharted journey? Perhaps this is why he sang with the remaining Apostles and offered a "prayer unto God."

President David O. McKay wrote, "I am reminded that just before the mob broke into Carthage Jail, just before the bullets ended the mortal existence of Hyrum the Patriarch and his brother Joseph the Prophet, the beautiful hymn, 'The Poor Wayfaring Man of Grief,' by Montgomery had echoed through those barricaded halls. Music in praise of Christ and in thanksgiving was the last impression on the spirit of Joseph Smith and of his brother, Hyrum."[5]

Is music important to the Lord? Evidently so. The Savior of the world and the Prophet of the Restoration both prepared for their last moments of mortality with it. Doctrine and Covenants 135:3 tells us that the Savior and Joseph Smith have done more for the salvation of men in this world than any other men who ever lived in it.

Many prophets of this dispensation have spoken explicitly of music as a missionary tool and as a tool to edify and uplift. President McKay once remarked, "There can be no greater missionary work than to sing the songs of Zion among our friends who have not yet accepted the message of the restored gospel."[6] President Heber J. Grant stated, "The singing of our sacred hymns, written by the servants of God, has a powerful effect in converting people to the principles of the Gospel, and in promoting peace and spiritual growth. Singing is a prayer to the Lord."[7]

President John Taylor wrote, "Music prevails in the heavens."[8] He also said, "The very spirit of religion is breathed into music. . . . Never, indeed, do we feel so near heaven as when listening to the performance of some grand anthem, in which the angels themselves might fitly take their parts."[9] If music prevails in the heavens, are mortals the originators of beautiful compositions, or are they simply translators of that which was already composed in more heavenly spheres? Is this divine origin of music the reason why it has such a powerful effect upon the spirit of man and why the Lord can use it for so much good? The First Presidency has said, "Inspirational music is an essential part of our church meetings. The hymns invite the Spirit of the Lord, create a feeling of reverence, unify us as members, and provide a way for us to offer praises to the Lord. Some of the greatest sermons are preached by the singing of hymns. Hymns move us to repentance and good works, build testimony and faith, comfort the weary, console the mourning, and inspire us to endure to the end."[10]

Elder Dallin H. Oaks, speaking about worship through music, stated:

> The singing of hymns is one of the best ways to put ourselves in tune with the Spirit of the Lord. . . .
>
> We need to make more use of our hymns to put us in tune with the Spirit of the Lord, to unify us, and to help us teach and learn our doctrine. We need to make better use of our hymns in missionary teaching, in gospel classes, in quorum meetings, in home evenings, and in home teaching visits. Music is an effective way to worship our Heavenly Father and his Son, Jesus Christ. We should use hymns when we need spiritual strength and inspiration.[11]

Once again, music is a prayer unto God. There is a saying taken from an old opera house that beautifully makes this point. It states, "God gave us music that we might pray without hands." Along these lines President George Albert Smith told a moving story about the power of music to touch the hearts of men:

> Many years ago, two humble elders laboring in the Southern States Mission were walking through the woods and finally came out into a clearing where there was a humble cottage, the home of friends who were not members of the Church. Overlooking this clearing was a hill covered by large trees. It had been a warm day, and when the elders arrived, instead of going into the house, they took their chairs out on the shady porch to visit with the family.

They didn't know that they were being watched or that danger threatened. They had come through a section of the country that was unfriendly, and having found a home where the family was friendly, they were grateful to the Lord for it.

They were asked to sing, and they selected the hymn, "Do What Is Right." And as they started to sing, there arrived on the brow of the hill above them a mob of armed horsemen. One of those men had previously threatened the missionaries and had kept watch for them on the road.

These armed men had come there with the determination to drive those missionaries out, but as they arrived at the top of the hill, they heard these missionaries singing. The leader of the mob dismounted and looked down among the trees and saw the roof of the house, but he could not see the elders. They continued to sing.

One by one the men got off their horses. One by one they removed their hats, and when the last note had died away and the elders had finished their singing, the men remounted their horses and rode away, and the leader said to his companions, "Men who sing like that are not the kind of men we have been told they are. These are good men."

The result was that the leader of the mob became converted to the Church and later was baptized. I never hear that hymn sung, but I think of that very unusual experience when two missionaries, under the infuence of the Spirit of God, turned the arms of the adversary away from them and brought repentance into the minds of those who had come to destroy them.[12]

Music is one of the most powerful ways that our Father can communicate to us. He can touch our hearts regardless of our language. There is no barrier. He may touch our emotions, our minds. He has always done so.

I think often of the incident related in 1 Samuel 16:14–23. An evil spirit had attacked Saul, the king of Israel. His servants suggested that they find someone who was a "cunning player on an harp" and play for Saul whenever the evil spirit was upon him. David, the son of Jesse the Bethlehemite, was the one chosen for the task. "And it came to pass, when the evil spirit from God [JST: which was not from God] was upon Saul, that David took an harp, and played with his hand: so Saul was refreshed, and was well, and the evil spirit departed from him" (verse 23).

If beautiful, inspiring music can cause evil spirits to depart, as in this case with Saul and David, can uninspired, degrading, depressing music invite them in? Elder Boyd K. Packer answered this question.

> Someone said recently that no music could be degrading, that music in and of itself is harmless and innocent.
>
> If that be true, then there should be some explanation for circumstances where local leaders have provided a building—expansive, light, and inviting—and have assembled a party of young people dressed modestly, well-groomed, with manners to match. Then over-amplified sounds of hard music are introduced and an influence pours into the room that is repellent to the spirit of God.[13]

Most of us have, at one time or another, felt a change in spirit because of the kind of music played in a location or circumstance. Music will generally do what it is written to do. If it is intended to agitate or depress, most of the time it will. Or if it is intended to mellow or pacify, it will. For this reason we would never prepare for a sacrament meeting by singing or playing heavy metal or punk rock. Yet on the other hand we most likely would never prepare to participate in a football game by listening to the Mormon Tabernacle Choir.

Music is important to the Lord, and he uses it for good and to accomplish many of his spiritual purposes. Elder Packer has expressed how music has influenced him on occasion. He also gives some wise counsel to those gifted in this area:

> I have been in places where I felt insecure and unprepared. I have yearned inwardly in great agony for some power to pave the way or loosen my tongue, that an opportunity

would not be lost because of my weakness and inadequacy. On more than a few occasions my prayers have been answered by the power of inspired music. I have been lifted above myself and beyond myself when the Spirit of the Lord has poured in upon the meeting, drawn there by beautiful, appropriate music. I stand indebted to the gifted among us who have that unusual sense of spiritual propriety.

Go to, then, you who are gifted; cultivate your gift. Develop it in any of the arts and in every worthy example of them. If you have the ability and the desire, seek a career or employ your talent as an avocation or cultivate it as a hobby. But in all ways bless others with it. Set a standard of excellence. Employ it in the secular sense to every worthy advantage, but never use it profanely. Never express your gift unworthily. Increase our spiritual heritage in music, in art, in literature, in dance, in drama.

When we have done it our activities will be a standard to the world. And our worship and devotion will remain as unique from the world as the Church is different from the world. Let the use of your gift be an expression of your devotion to Him who has given it to you. We who do not share in it will set a high standard of expectation: "For of him unto whom much is given much is required" (D&C 82:3).[14]

Satan is well aware of this powerful medium and is trying desperately to distort it and use it to his advantage. Again, remember that the major issue when it comes to music is the importance of our ability to receive revelation. We need to make wholesome music of all kinds a part of our lives. Secular music may be inspiring in many ways, but it will not allow us to feel the Spirit with the same power as will sacred music. We must not forget the warning of President Packer: "Some music is spiritually very destructive. You young people know what kind that is. The tempo, the sounds, and the lifestyle of those who perform it repel the Spirit. It is far more dangerous than you may suppose, for it can smother your spiritual senses."[15]

Not every spirit, or vision, or singing, is of God.
The devil is an orator; he is powerful.
—*Joseph Smith*

4

Opposition in All Things

A few years ago I had the opportunity to teach seminary at Timpview High School in Provo, Utah. I was excited to begin a new year and looked forward with great anticipation to what the future held. I was somewhat apprehensive, however, about going to Timpview, because it would be my first experience teaching or being at school without spending my afternoons playing football or baseball or coaching. I knew I could do it, but I worried nevertheless.

I suppose that is why I enjoyed pep assemblies so much. It was an opportunity to feel many of the same feelings I had had as a player and as a coach. You have probably had the same experience—chills running down your arms and the back of your neck when you enter the gymnasium while the band is playing and the cheerleaders are cheering. It's exciting!

I remember one particular assembly before a big game. The cheerleaders had planned a special class competition involving cream pies. The details are vague, but I do remember that some of the athletes—you know the type, the ones who all sit together and won't cheer except on rare occasions—got an idea to liven things up. The pies never ended up in the contest but on the cheerleaders.

As far as I am aware, the cheerleaders said very little to these young men. Each girl allowed the boys to think they had really gained the upper hand and gotten away with a fast one. The pies were soon forgotten, and another pep assembly greeted us a few weeks later. This time as we entered the gym we saw twelve carameled apples on the floor at center court—big, beautiful, brown carameled apples, waiting for someone to eat them.

When everyone was settled down and the band had ceased playing, the head cheerleader walked to the micro-phone and began to explain that morning's class competition. From a small piece of paper she read the names of some of the football players who had been involved in the pie incident, as well as some other young men, and challenged them to a candied-apple-eating contest. As each name was read, the cor-responding young man came down to the basketball court with confidence, raising his hands in triumph, knowing that he could eat an apple faster than any girl.

Another teacher and I were called upon to judge this his-toric event. The cheerleaders explained the rules to me, and I then explained them to the young men. The young men, how-ever, were not overly concerned, because each was proficient in eating, and in eating quickly. The only two rules were: (1) every apple on each team must be completely devoured, and (2) the girls were to be allowed a ten-second head start.

After hearing the rules, the young men decided on a game plan. They would not chew—just bite, swallow, bite, swallow, until each apple was gone. With such strategy the contest began.

The whistle blew, and the girls began to eat with great care and deliberate actions. The boys, on the other hand, stood watching, waiting for their winning opportunity.

When the second whistle blew, each young man, without any hesitation or forethought, lunged toward the carameled apple before him. With no table manners evident, they began to devour them with great haste—bite, swallow, bite, swallow. Then suddenly, in unison, as if a light switch had been turned on inside each boy, their heads raised in shock and disbelief as they realized they were not eating candy-covered apples but candy-covered onions! The crowd roared when they realized what had happened. The cheerleaders, on the other hand, stood calmly, hands signaling the two-fingered peace sign in recognition of their sly plan to deceive the football players.

By now these poor boys were looking as white as sheets and trying to get rid of the large bites of raw onion which were now floating throughout their systems. I'll never forget it! Those poor guys smelled like onions for quite some time, and it was not an easy task to rid themselves of the stench.

Since then I have thought very seriously about what happened that day at Timpview, and I have told that story hundreds of times while speaking about music and its relationship to our actions, feelings, thoughts, and spirituality. The cheerleaders had made the onions appear so much like the apples that the football players could not tell the difference until the onions became a part of them and it was too late.

No one ever dreamed that those sweet young cheerleaders would be so mischievous as to use something these young men loved so dearly—food—to get back at and deceive them.

When I ponder that story I always ask myself, Would Satan try to do the same thing to deceive us? Would he use the things we love the most to bring us down to destruction? Would he even use music, which most of us love dearly, to lead us astray?

In Doctrine and Covenants 50:2–3 the Lord told the elders of the Church that one of Satan's major objectives is to deceive us: "Behold, verily I say unto you, that there are many spirits which are false spirits, which have gone forth in the earth, deceiving the world. And also Satan hath sought to deceive you, that he might overthrow you." He is the champion of all liars and does not care one bit about you or me. His only desire is to seek our misery.

Of course he would use music! Elder Bruce R. McConkie

wisely warned, "Unfortunately not all music is good and edify-ing. Lucifer uses much that goes by the name of music to lead people to that which does not edify and is not of God. Just as language can be used to bless or curse, so music is a means of singing praises to the Lord or of planting evil thoughts and de-sires in the minds of men."[1] Without question Satan knows that music is one of God's greatest tools for good. Without question he is aware that it is one of the most important and powerful influences in our lives. Would he not use music, then, as one of his greatest counterfeits?

Of course Satan would use music to his advantage if he could. Second Nephi 2:11 states, "For it must needs be, that there is an opposition in all things." To me that means that whenever God creates something good, true, and beautiful, Satan, in his devious way, comes up with something false, counterfeit, and ugly, yet which appears to be similar to our Father's creation. He acts, if you will, in much the same man-ner that the cheerleaders did with the onions. He tries to de-ceive us into partaking of music or music videos that are false, counterfeit, and ugly in hopes that we will not detect it until it is a part of us or until it is too late altogether.

If there were no opposition we would have no freedom of choice. Without freedom to choose we would have a very dif-ficult time existing. In fact, as the prophet Lehi taught, there would be no purpose in our creation. There would be no righteousness because there would be no wickedness, and if there were no righteousness, there would be no happiness. (See 2 Nephi 2:13.) We must have opposites. We must have choice.

How do many of us feel when we are forced to do some-thing? Many of us rebel because we do not like to be told every single thing that we should do. As mentioned earlier, when a parent yells down the hall for a teenager to "turn that garbage down," it's easy for the teenager to turn the volume up instead. It is not necessarily right, but so often it is the case. Without the freedom of choice, we lose our valuable gift of agency.

The essence of agency was taught to me by a great teacher

when he said, "To tell is to preach. To ask is to teach." Perhaps this is why the Savior said, "Come, follow me," not forcing or pushing, but inviting and then leading the way.

With this agency we must also realize that there is deep and heavy responsibility. The Lord instructed us in section 58 of the Doctrine and Covenants that we are agents unto ourselves. We are free to choose. If we have to be commanded in all things we are slothful and unwise servants, wherefore we receive no reward (see D&C 58:26). Lehi instructed us in a very similar manner in 2 Nephi 2:27: "Wherefore, men are free according to the flesh; and all things are given them which are expedient unto man. And they are free to choose liberty and eternal life, through the great Mediator of all men, or to choose captivity and death, according to the captivity and power of the devil; for he seeketh that all men might be miserable like unto himself." It seems obvious that the Lord has allowed us to choose for ourselves but has not taken away the responsibility for the choice.

Elder Bernard P. Brockbank, former Assistant to the Quorum of the Twelve, has said:

> Young people, do you think Satan has music in his program? Do you think the Lord has music in his program? Satan's music has a way of destroying the godliness within a human soul, and there is some of the hard rock music that is definitely not from the Lord. It will tear down your spiritual strength and your divine nature. Don't get involved in it. When you feel that rhythm of hard rock music becoming part and fiber of your soul, get away from it while you are young enough. Just remember Satan will try to lure you away with conniving and deceitful practices so that you hardly know you are walking down the road with him.[2]

Joseph Addison, English essayist and poet, said, "Music is the only sensual gratification in which mankind may indulge to excess without injury to their moral or religious feelings."[3] Perhaps that was true in his day, but is it in ours? Some of today's music appears to have moved away from such innocence. It is difficult for some to accept the idea that some music is "bad." There seems to be a common philosophy in today's world that music is only bad if the listener perceives it as such. However, our prophets and Apostles have taught us otherwise. Elder David B. Haight of the Quorum of the Twelve Apostles said to Aaronic priesthood holders, "You are different [from the rest of the world]. Pornography, filthy literature and movies, vile language, and suggestive music are not part of your life. They can destroy you."[4]

Obtaining and recognizing the Spirit is perhaps the most essential asset in determining that music which will have a beneficial effect upon us. In Jacob 4:13 we learn that "the Spirit speaketh the truth and lieth not. Wherefore, it speaketh of things as they really are, and of things as they really will be." If we have the Spirit we will see things as they really are and not just as they appear on the outside. I know of no greater guide that could be given to anyone for detecting Satan's ways. We cannot forget that "that which doth not edify is not of God, and is darkness" (D&C 50:23).

Many, many years ago, before any of us came to earth, an incident took place that may help us understand why Satan would take musical apples and counterfeit them into musical onions to be used for destructive purposes. This event is commonly referred to as the War in Heaven.

> And there was war in heaven: Michael and his angels fought against the dragon; and the dragon fought and his angels, . . .
>
> And the great dragon was cast out, that old serpent, called the Devil, and Satan, which deceiveth the whole world: he was cast out into the earth, and his angels were cast out with him. . . .
>
> Therefore rejoice, ye heavens, and ye that dwell in them. Woe to the inhabiters of the earth and of the sea! for the devil is come down unto you, having great wrath, because he knoweth that he hath but a short time.

And the dragon was wroth with the woman [the church of Jesus Christ], and went to make war with the remnant of her seed, which keep the commandments of God, and have the testimony of Jesus Christ. (Revelation 12:7, 9, 12, 17.)

From studying these passages of scripture, it seems obvious that Satan is trying to concentrate his attack on those who are striving to do good and who have testimonies of Jesus Christ. He wants to destroy the strong before they become an opposition to him here as they were in the War in Heaven.

> Lucifer desires all good people. He even tempted the Savior on at least three recorded occasions. . . .
> Satan wants all men, but especially is he anxious for the leading men who have influence. Perhaps he might try much harder to claim men who are likely to be his greatest opposition, men in high places who could persuade many others not to become servants to Satan.
> It seems that missionaries are special targets. . . . Satan takes a special interest in all such workers.[5]

Satan still remembers the premortal existence and is aware of those individuals who fought most valiantly against him, and he "walketh about, seeking whom he may devour" (1 Peter 5:8). He drew a third of the host of heaven with him (see Revelation 12:4), and when they were cast out, that third of the host of heaven came to earth and brought with them the knowledge they had previously possessed. Our knowledge, on the other hand, was temporarily taken from us through our birth into mortality.

As Elder LeGrand Richards pointed out, perhaps this is why at the time of the birth of the great prophet Moses, the adversary put it into the heart of Pharaoh to have all the baby boys drowned in the River Nile. He obviously knew that if he did not kill Moses the baby, he would have to deal with Moses the prophet.

In the meridian of time, when Jesus was born into the

world, Satan put it into the heart of Herod to have all of the young children within his jurisdiction who were under the age of two killed in hopes of destroying Jesus the baby so that he did not have to deal with Jesus the Messiah, the Redeemer, the Son of God.

Later, in the spring of 1820 when Joseph Smith was but fourteen years of age, he went into a grove of trees and a power of darkness rested upon him. It continued, as Elder Richards described it, "until Joseph felt like it would crush the very life out of his body; but through his prayer, finally a pillar of light descended and he was released from the power of Satan. Satan knew that he would have to reckon with that man Joseph Smith because he was one of those noble and great ones that God said he would make his rulers."[6]

Were many of today's youth with Moses, the Savior, and the Prophet Joseph Smith as part of the "noble and great ones" spoken of by Abraham? (See Abraham 3:22.) Is this why Satan is trying so desperately to destroy them? Will they become "leading men and women who have influence?" Perhaps this is why it seems that "all hell has broken loose" and why it is so difficult to carry on in doing good continually.

This is one of the major reasons I shiver when I hear young people or their parents say, "Oh, come on now, it doesn't really matter what I listen to, does it? I mean, after all, I'm more mature for my age and I can handle it." How often have you heard, "It doesn't affect me the way it does other people"? How often have those famous last words "I can handle it" been spoken just before disaster or sorrow disassembled a once happy, flowering life?

If the adversary can convince us that it makes little difference what we listen to, watch, or take into our systems, then we have become his. We have become as King Benjamin said: "That ye do withdraw yourselves from the Spirit of the Lord, that it may have no place in you to guide you in wisdom's paths that ye may be blessed, prospered, and preserved" (Mosiah 2:36). It does make a difference. I marvel that young people or parents would ever consider fighting Satan on his territory. It terrifies me. Can they honestly feel they have a chance to survive?

George Albert Smith said:

> My grandfather used to say to his family, "There is a line of demarkation, well defined, between the Lord's territory and the devil's. If you will stay on the Lord's side of the line, you will be under his influence and will have no desire to do wrong; but if you cross to the devil's side of the line one inch, you are in the tempter's power, and if he is successful, you will not be able to think or even reason properly, because you will have lost the Spirit of the Lord."[7]

It is hoped that all parents will show as much interest in the CDs, tapes, and videos their children purchase as they would the reading material they bring into the home. Most parents would not allow their children to purchase pornographic magazines or videos, yet sometimes they unknowingly provide money for music that can be every bit as damaging in its influence.

Can we continue to walk day after day through a spiritual mire of inappropriate entertainment and remain unscathed? If we choose to make unwise decisions in our entertainment, it cannot help but have a direct relationship on our actions, feelings, thoughts, and spirituality.

May the reader who feels that it makes little difference what type of music is listened to be reminded of what Doctrine and Covenants 76:25–26 tells us—that Satan was so powerful in the premortal existence that he "was in authority in the presence of God," and that when he was cast out of God's presence "the heavens wept over him."

Satan has spent thousands of years learning the weaknesses of men. We as mortals are shortsighted when we believe that after a few short years on earth, with no knowledge of what went on before, we are a match for the likes of him. Nephi wrote about what happened to his brothers and the sons of Ishmael and also their wives when they gave little thought to what music and other forms of entertainment they participated in. He wrote, "After we had been driven forth before the wind for the space of many days, behold, my brethren and the sons of Ishmael and also their wives began to make themselves merry, insomuch that they began to dance, and to sing, and to speak with much rudeness [*rudeness* being interpreted as "harsh, coarse, crude, or vulgar"], yea, even that they did forget by what power they had been brought thither; yea, they were lifted up unto exceeding rudeness" (1 Nephi 18:9).

I am not saying that if we listen to certain kinds of music we will become involved in the negative behaviors being suggested. For example, if you watch a sexually explicit video or movie, you will not necessarily commit immoral acts. If you listen to music that promotes drug use, you will not necessarily become involved in drugs. Or if you listen to music performed by those involved in witchcraft, devil worship, or the occult, you probably will not abandon your religious faith and become involved in such practices. If your favorite music promotes suicide, the odds are you will not necessarily commit suicide. But what if you become so desensitized that you lose your ability to feel deep spiritual feelings? What if you no longer are shocked or offended by some of these negative behaviors, because they have become so commonplace in your thought processes and in your daily experience? Or what if you simply lose the desire to pray, search the scriptures, serve a mission, or marry in the temple? Again, I'm not saying that inappropriate music will directly cause you to sin, but if you stop doing the most important things in your life, have you not been negatively affected?

As has been expressed so often by Church leaders, we cannot hold hands with Satan and God at the same time. We have to let go of one or the other. When we worship certain types of music or any other worldly idol more than spiritual things, we are holding hands with Satan and are walking in darkness. The chances are greater then that we will become insensitive to spiritual things. We may become as Laman and Lemuel, who had seen an angel and had heard the voice of the Lord from time to time, but when the still small voice spoke, they were "past feeling" and could not "feel his words" (1 Nephi 17:45). Doubts and fears will cloud our minds. We will begin to walk in our own way, after the image of our own god, "whose image is in the likeness of the world, and whose substance is that of an idol" (D&C 1:16). If we lose our desire to be missionaries, to read scriptures, to pray, to marry in the temple as commanded, have we not then been drastically or even fatally affected by the music? We must cling to the iron rod and follow the prophets of God. The great prophet Isaiah may have seen our modern-day problem with music and "partying" when he said, "Wo unto them that rise up early in the morning, that they may follow strong drink, that continue until night, and wine inflame them! And the harp, and the viol, the tabret, and pipe, and wine are in their feasts; but they regard not the work of the Lord, neither consider the operation of his hands." (2 Nephi 15:11–12.)

Things are not the same as in years past. When it comes to music and most other areas, the differences between the world and the Church appears wider in our day than ever before. A "good versus evil" scenario is being acted out before us. Satan is employing his forces against all that is good. But as President David O. McKay has said, those who follow gospel teachings and practice self-control "will stand as beacon lights whose rays will penetrate a sin-stained world."[8]

As each of us fights this constant battle with the evil one concerning music or videos or movies and every other facet of our lives, may we keep in mind and treasure the words of Elders Robert L. Backman, Vaughn J Featherstone, and Rex D. Pinegar. This message was given to all young men in the Church, but I believe it can apply to young women as well.

We live in a great and evil day. Never have the powers of darkness, evil, and perversion covered the earth as they do in this generation. This is a season in the Lord's affairs that the greatest generation of young men in the history of the world is being called forth. Our work is at hand. It is not a time for cowardice or compromise nor is it a time to indulge or live an undisciplined life. It is a time to rally to the banner of our Master, to declare with unwavering allegiance our loyalty to His great cause. It is a time to be noble and pure, to live lives disciplined like no other generation. It is a season for a "Spartan" life, a "committed" life, a "conquering" life.

This generation of young men is going to do deeds never done before. You are going to accomplish the seemingly impossible because you are on His errand. Your generation will fight the greatest army of Satanic hosts ever assembled. You will be severely outnumbered. You will need a deep and abiding faith in Christ to survive—and you will survive. The Lord and His servants will triumph, we do know that.[9]

If, as suggested by these three General Authorities, the only way to overcome the spiritual slaughter taking place in our world today is to establish a deep and abiding faith in Christ, the question must be asked, Is your entertainment leading you to Christ or away from him? We must ponder deeply this question and be honest with ourselves. With music being such a powerful medium for good or evil, we had better learn how to make the right and appropriate decisions. We must learn to choose between the musical apples and the musical onions.

Of every tree of the garden thou mayest freely eat,
but of the tree of the knowledge of good and evil,
thou shall not eat of it, nevertheless,
thou mayest choose for thyself, for it is given unto thee.
—Moses 3:16–17

5

Making the
Music Decision

As a teacher I believe in the philosophy that says, "If you give a man a fish, he has food for a day. Teach that man to fish, and he has food for the rest of his life."

As a teacher, father, and priesthood leader, I have pondered deeply over that saying. It has greatly influenced me. In fact, it reminds me of a story about a fleet of fishing boats that docked each afternoon for years at the same pier. Each day as they entered the dock, the ship hands would clean their fish and throw the remains into the water. The seagulls in the area would flock each evening to the pier, hoping to find dinner and take part of it back to their young.

For years the seagulls obtained plenty of food. They never had to work for themselves. The fishermen provided everything. As a result, the seagulls never learned to fish.

Then one day the fishermen and their ships did not return to the familiar pier but went in search of more fertile waters. As a result, the seagulls missed their evening meal. Days passed, and no ships—thus, no fish. Each day brought death to large numbers of birds. Eventually most of the seagulls in the region died. They had been hand-fed for so long that they had not learned one of the most basic and simple elements of life—to feed themselves!

Have we become like the birds at the pier? Do we want so much for someone else to tell us what we should and shouldn't listen to or watch that we do not learn the most basic and simple procedures for making our own decisions and choices?

It is likely that many may criticize this approach and may feel that it is very important to have all of the details, including a specific list of groups and stars to avoid. However, each person can learn to choose for him- or herself, without a current pop music chart, if he or she will not be afraid of the truth and will learn to apply correct principles. As mentioned earlier, so often when we get caught up in the specifics it is very easy to encourage the very thing we try to prevent because we talk about it too much and in too much detail. We incite and inspire ideas that perhaps were previously not even thought of by the listener. We invoke or titillate curiosity.

What would happen if I gave the reader a list of what I thought was appropriate and inappropriate music? How long would the list be current? By the time this book was published the list would be outdated. Another problem that arises is that you would simply have my opinion. As discussed earlier in the book, my opinion means little, because it may not be entirely correct. Think for a moment what may happen when the youth of today become the parents of tomorrow and their children come to them saying, "Mom, Dad, you gotta listen to this music! It's the greatest music you've ever heard!" Will they respond as their parents may have done? "You call that music? I can't understand a single word they're saying! How do you listen to that garbage? And how can you listen to anyone who dresses so stupid? Sit down. Back when I was your age I read a book that told me all about Madonna, Crash Test Dummies, and the Cranberries," and so on and so on. They'll look at you and say, "Crash Test who? Yeah, we know. That was back be-

fore they invented water and when you used to have to ride
your dinosaur to school uphill both ways. Yeah, we know all
about it!" They won't have a clue what is being talked about.
Do any of you young readers know anything about Perry
Como or Dean Martin? Why not? They sold almost as many
records in their day as many of the popular groups today combined. Yet many of us know very little about them because
they were popular many years ago. Do you really think it will
be much different in the future?

As was previously mentioned, one of the major problems
with music seems to be choosing between the "apples" and
the "onions." There is much that is good and beautiful. There
is also much that is false, counterfeit, and ugly, yet appears to
be good.

How does a person choose? Perhaps one of the greatest
blessings we enjoy in this life is the fact that our Father in
Heaven has not left us alone to make these difficult decisions.
He teaches us how to fish so that we may continually provide
"food" for ourselves.

The scriptures and the teachings of Church leaders are
filled with ways of helping us to evaluate music and then
choose for ourselves. We must learn to follow the direction of
the Lord or we, like the young football players at Timpview,
may partake of the "onions" and not even be aware of it.

Satan has done such a masterful job in counterfeiting his
music that without some assistance it is not an easy task to dis-
tinguish the "apples" from the "onions." For this reason it is
important to use eternal principles rather than the specifics of
the day to make our choices. The artists may change, but these
principles never change. "What I the Lord have spoken, I have
spoken, and I excuse not myself; and though the heavens and
the earth pass away, my word shall not pass away, but shall all
be fulfilled, whether by mine own voice or by the voice of my
servants, it is the same" (D&C 1:38).

The book of Moroni provides us with perhaps one of the
clearest ways the Lord has provided for us to discern Satan
and his counterfeits. This passage teaches us that we may

know the difference between good and evil just as assuredly
as we know the difference between night and day.

> Wherefore, all things which are good cometh of God; and
> that which is evil cometh of the devil; for the devil is an
> enemy unto God, and fighteth against him continually, and
> inviteth and enticeth to sin, and to do that which is evil con-
> tinually.
>
> But behold, that which is of God inviteth and enticeth to
> do good continually; wherefore, every thing which inviteth
> and enticeth to do good, and to love God, and to serve him,
> is inspired of God.
>
> Wherefore, take heed, my beloved brethren, that ye do
> not judge that which is evil to be of God, or that which is
> good and of God to be of the devil.
>
> For behold, my brethren, it is given unto you to judge,
> that ye may know good from evil; and the way to judge is as
> plain, that ye may know with a perfect knowledge, as the
> daylight is from the dark night.
>
> For behold, the Spirit of Christ is given to every man, that
> he may know good from evil; wherefore, I show unto you the
> way to judge; for every thing which inviteth to do good, and
> to persuade to believe in Christ, is sent forth by the power
> and gift of Christ; wherefore ye may know with a perfect
> knowledge it is of God.
>
> But whatsoever thing persuadeth men to do evil, and be-
> lieve not in Christ, and deny him, and serve not God, then ye
> may know with a perfect knowledge it is of the devil; for after
> this manner doth the devil work, for he persuadeth no man to
> do good, no, not one; neither do his angels; neither do they
> who subject themselves unto him. (Moroni 7:12–17.)

Again, never fearing truth becomes the key. The prophet
Mormon, as he spoke these words to the people in the syna-
gogue, obviously had a specific purpose for telling us in verse
16 that this is "the" way and not simply "a" way of choosing
between good and evil. It also seems clear that verse 17 is not
necessarily saying that all music must be of a religious nature

in order to be good or appropriate. There is much of today's music that we may well enjoy if we avoid certain types.

President Ezra Taft Benson stated, "We encourage you to listen to uplifting music, both popular and classical, that builds the spirit."[1] Again, I need not go down a list of groups that are good and bad. Verse 17 has the answer. If our music persuades us to do evil and believe not in Christ and deny him and serve not God, in any way, regardless of how much we enjoy it, how popular it is, or who performs it, we know with a perfect knowledge it is not of God but is of the devil and has as its purpose to desensitize us, blur our spiritual vision, and destroy our ability to receive revelation.

President Gordon B. Hinckley has taught us, "Some would have us believe that the area between good and evil is largely gray and that it is difficult to determine what is right and what is wrong. For any who so believe, I recommend this beautiful statement of Moroni found in the Book of Mormon." He then quoted Moroni 7:16. Continuing on, he said, "Let us establish in our lives the habit of reading those things which will strengthen our faith in the Lord Jesus Christ, the Savior of the world. He is the pivotal figure of our theology and our faith."[2]

Let us likewise establish in our lives the habit of listening to that music or watching those videos that will strengthen our faith in the Lord Jesus Christ, or that at least will not damage our faith. Making this decision is sometimes difficult. It is also important to realize that if we take away that which is inappropriate, we must replace it with something good or we'll go right back to that which we abandoned. In an age where there are so many voices, which one will we choose to follow? As Sister Elaine Cannon has so beautifully put it, "Since there are so many voices around us, it seems vital that we hear His!"[3] However, if we're going to make these appropriate decisions we must be somewhat educated in the process.

In considering the counsel given in Moroni chapter 7 there are some very important things to remember. Larry Bastian, former chairman of the Church Youth Music Committee, has commented,

There are at least three important persons who participate in each musical experience. First is the composer, who writes the melody and suggests a harmonic and rhythmic treatment. That which he seeks to communicate is then interpreted by an arranger or performer, who may treat the music in such a fashion as to communicate exactly the opposite from that intended by the composer.

The third important person is the listener. Our musical tastes are the result of conditioning and personal experience. Every person responds to music, then, in his own unique fashion.

The key to discerning the quality of music lies in what it communicates to us individually and personally. Perhaps we Latter-day Saints have not often enough asked ourselves the question: "What does this music say to me?" Considering the influence of evil in the affairs of today's world, especially in contemporary entertainment, we should ask it often.

If one can answer that a song is spiritually inspiring or that it urges him to see himself in a more noble perspective, then that music is good. If the music just entertains or momentarily lifts the spirits, then it has a useful place. If it makes him want to respond in a carnal, sensual way or to consider unrighteous desires, then that music should be avoided.

Sometimes the environment in which music is heard has an effect of its own. For example, a song that sounds pleasant and refreshing on the stereo at home may make a different impression in a remote corner of a darkened room with the music at a blaring level.

Music is the language of the heart and of the spirit. It often communicates on a level where words are inadequate. It is on this level that it must be evaluated. We may not understand sometimes why we respond as we do, but we should measure the response, choose that which is compatible with our understanding of the eternal nature of things, and reject the rest.[4]

Another important standard to use while making a decision on music is the thirteenth article of faith:

We believe in being honest, true, chaste, benevolent, virtuous, and in doing good to all men; indeed, we may say that we follow the admonition of Paul—We believe all things, we hope all things, we have endured many things, and hope to be able to endure all things. If there is anything virtuous, lovely, or of good report or praiseworthy, we seek after these things.

Is our music virtuous, lovely, of good report, or praiseworthy? If it is, wonderful! It is good, and we'll never go wrong by listening to it. On the other hand, if it is not, then we know with a perfect knowledge, as the daylight is from the dark night, that it is not of God and should not be part of our lives. Does it persuade us to be honest, true, chaste, benevolent, and virtuous and to do good to all men? If so, again, wonderful. If not, we certainly know where it comes from.

A third important way of choosing is found in Doctrine and Covenants 50:23–25, which reads, "And that which doth not edify is not of God, and is darkness. That which is of God is light; and he that receiveth light, and continueth in God, receiveth more light; and that light groweth brighter and brighter until the perfect day. And again, verily I say unto you, and I say it that you may know the truth, that you may chase darkness from among you."

Perhaps chasing this darkness from among us is one of life's greatest challenges. However, if we will but apply the correct and eternal principles taught in this chapter we will better understand why we make the choices we make and what Omni 1:25 means when it says, "For there is nothing which is good save it comes from the Lord: and that which is evil cometh from the devil."

President Spencer W. Kimball counseled, "We cannot give in to the ways of the world with regard to the realm of art. . . . Brigham Young said there is 'no music in hell.' Our art must be the kind which edifies man, which takes into account his immortal nature, and which prepares us for heaven, not hell."[5]

Elder Boyd K. Packer has said:

Our youth have been brought up on a diet of music that is loud and fast, more intended to agitate than to pacify, more intended to excite than to calm. Even so, there is a breadth of it, some soft enough to be innocent and appealing to our youth, and that which is hard, and that is where the problem is. . . . The music of the drug and the hard rock culture . . . has little virtue and it is repellent to the Spirit of God. . . .

. . . There is much of today's music that they may well enjoy, if they avoid the hard kind.[6]

Did the prophet Moroni have some of today's music and videos in mind when he said, "And again I would exhort you that ye would come unto Christ, and lay hold upon every good gift, and touch not the evil gift, nor the unclean thing" (Moroni 10:30)? Elder H. Burke Peterson in his last address as a General Authority said he felt that Moroni did. He taught in a general conference priesthood session:

My thoughts will center on our sometimes innocent involvement in one of the terrible, unclean things referred to by this ancient prophet. Satan, the very devil and father of all lies, has slyly and slowly lowered the social norms of morality to a tragic and destructive level. In magazines and books, on CDs and tapes, on our television and theater screens is portrayed more and more often a lifestyle that might even rival the excesses of those who lived in Sodom and Gomorrah. The screens, music, and printed materials, etc., are filled with a profusion of sex, nudity, and vulgarity.

One of the great tragedies is that too many men and boys who hold the priesthood of God are watching and listening to this type of so-called entertainment. Some do it only casually at first. They think they are spiritually strong and will be immune to its influence. This trash is nothing more nor less than pornography dressed in one of its many imitation robes of splendor—one of the master counterfeiter's best products.

Part of the tragedy I speak of is that many men and boys do not recognize they are trapped or soon will be. Unfortunately, I fear even some within the sound of my voice have an addiction and do not realize it. They see this as a form of entertainment that serves as a relief from the troubles of the day. In point of fact and in reality, *it is only relieving them of their spirituality* and their capacity to draw on the powers of heaven in times of need. . . .

Brethren, I plead with you to leave it alone. Stay away from any movie, video, publication, or music—*regardless of its rating*—where illicit behavior and expressions are a part of the action. Have the courage to turn it off in your living room. Throw the tapes and the publications in the garbage can, for that is where we keep garbage.

. . . It is my understanding that any time we look at or listen to the kind of material we have been speaking of—even in its mildest form—the light inside of us grows dimmer because the darkness inside increases. The effect of this is that we cannot think as clearly on life's challenges—be they business, church, school, family, or personal—because the channel to the source of all light for the solving of problems is cluttered with various unclean images. Our entitlement to personal revelation on any subject is severely restricted. We don't do as well in school or at work. We are left more on our own, and as a result we make more mistakes and we are not as happy. Remember, our mind is a wonderful instrument. It will record and keep whatever we put into it, both trash and beauty. When we see or hear anything filthy or vulgar, whatever the source, our mind records it, and as it makes the filthy record, beauty and clean thoughts are pushed into the background. Hope and faith in Christ begin to fade, and more and more, turmoil and discontent become our companions. . . .

Again I say, leave it alone. Turn it off, walk away from it, burn it, erase it, destroy it. I know it is hard counsel we give when we say movies that are R-rated, and many with PG-13 ratings, are produced by satanic influences. Our standards should not be dictated by the rating system. I repeat, because of what they *really* represent, these types of movies, music, tapes, etc. serve the purposes of the author of all darkness.

Brethren, let's consider again why we cannot be involved in Satan's program of entertainment and be held guiltless.

Why? Because *we are men and boys of the covenant,* and that makes us different from all others. When we've made a covenant with the Lord, we are special—not ordinary, but special. He loves all of his sons, *but those of the covenant have a special responsibility.*[7]

Now that we have some appropriate and surefire ways of choosing, let's put our knowledge to use by asking ourselves four specific questions:

1. *Lyrics.* What if the music is appropriate and meets the above criteria for choosing good music, but the words or lyrics are inappropriate or contrary to the teachings of Christ? Can the song be good, and should we listen to it? Often when I speak on this subject, parents will say, "Well, I can't understand a single word they say anyway. How do they listen to that stuff?" The younger people generally respond with, "I don't listen to the words. I just like the rhythm and the beat."

It has been discovered that it makes little difference, to most, if you understand the words or if you even pay attention to them. For many, the minute words are put together with music they're cemented into the memory. It's amazing how we often sing or hum tunes with words that we would never dream of speaking. It's also amazing how many students have a difficult time memorizing facts and information, but they know every word of every Top 40 song. I love the simple phrase, "A song will outlive all sermons in the memory."

Have you ever stopped to consider why the characters of *Sesame Street* almost always use music to teach the children? A young mind simply can assimilate and remember information better when it is put to a catchy rhythm and beat. Big Bird, Cookie Monster, and the Count always use music. "One, two, three, four, *A* is for agua! . . ." Even Barney the Dinosaur uses music to say, "I love you, you love me. . . ." You'll never forget it, even if you hate it!

Think about how you learned your ABCs. Was it through music? Of course, and the tune was "Twinkle, Twinkle, Little Star." Amazing!

While thumbing through a local sales brochure one day I noticed that it gave some interesting figures. "Children remember 10 percent heard, 40 percent story, 60 percent visual aids, and 90 percent that is taught by music. Teach your children through music." If these figures are accurate, it is obvious that words accompanied by music play a far greater role in our lives than most of us have ever imagined.

Some time ago I was driving down the freeway with my radio playing when a song by the Beatles came on. In an instant my mind rushed back to the late '60s, and I began to daydream while singing and pondering. I caught hold of some pleasant memories from my past and remembered some activities I had participated in while listening to that song so many years before. As I sang, I never even missed a comma. I remembered every single word. It had been at least ten to twelve years since I had heard that song, but the lyrics were vivid in my memory.

President Joseph F. Smith taught,

> May I say to you that in reality a man cannot forget anything? He may have a lapse of memory; he may not be able to recall at the moment a thing that he knows, or words that he has spoken; he may not have the power at his will to call up these events and words; but let God Almighty touch the mainspring of the memory, and awaken recollection, and you will find then that you have not even forgotten a single idle word that you have spoken! I believe the word of God to be true, and, therefore, I warn the youth of Zion, as well as those who are advanced in years, to beware of saying wicked things, of speaking evil, and taking in vain the name of sacred things and sacred beings. Guard your words, that you may not offend even man, much less offend God.[8]

It's easy to say that the words are not important or that they're not the major part of a song. However, when they are constantly in our minds it's hard to throw out the scriptural teaching that as a man "thinketh in his heart, so is he"

(Proverbs 23:7). In fact, I believe we are as much what we listen to or watch as we are what we eat. The only difference is that instead of the material coming into our bodies by way of the mouth, it enters through our eyes and ears. It becomes a part of us! Becoming what we think about most of the time is not a new concept to the advertising industry. Very few commercials on television or radio are not accompanied by catchy jingles or memorable musical scores.

The *Wall Street Journal* printed an interesting article concerning advertisers using musical groups to reach young consumers. The findings were remarkable. For years advertisers wanted nothing to do with the flamboyance of the rock industry. However, it didn't take long for them to change their minds when dollars were involved. Most rock stars are much more business oriented now than in times past, and money is the name of the game. For this purpose many advertisers have used rock 'n' roll to sell their products. Oftentimes they use the music for songs from the '60s, '70s, and '80s in their jingles so that the consumer will immediately recognize it.[9]

With the advent of music videos, lyrics have become extremely important in the selling of products. If Saturday morning advertisers can sell a box of cereal in thirty seconds, can music promoters sell us a lifestyle in a three-minute video?

With MTV and other video stations the shape of fashion has changed in the United States. It has made extreme clothing totally acceptable. Outrageous clothing that would have taken possibly fifteen years to get visibility now is popular within a week because of its use in videos.[10]

Simply put, the lyrics do make a difference and are programmed into our minds whether we like it or not. Very few of us purposefully memorize the words to daily television or radio commercials. But with repetition, they often become a part of us, programmed into our thought patterns by their connection with unforgettable tunes. For example, I love to ask adults to fill in the blanks of a commercial that hasn't been on TV since the early 1970s. They almost always know it but haven't thought about it for years. It goes, "Winston tastes

good like a _____ should." Did you get it? What if I use another old commercial such as: "You deserve a _____ today, so
get up and _____ _____ to _____." Did you get that one?
Chances are you probably did. But do you know any of the
details of any commercial selling insurance to those over age
sixty-five? If you are like most people, you probably don't.
Why? Probably because most insurance commercials for those
over sixty-five don't have one note played in them. They don't
want young people to remember to buy insurance before they
get older, or the company makes no money! It does make a
difference what the lyrics are saying. Again, they do become a
part of us! Perhaps this is why President John Taylor remarked,
"If I had time to enter into this subject alone I could show you
upon scientific principles that man himself is a self-registering
machine, his eyes, his ears, his nose, the touch, the taste, and
all the various senses of the body, are so many media whereby
man lays up for himself a record."[11]

If the lyrics, then, are inappropriate or negative in nature
or contrary to the teachings of Christ in any way, I plead with
the reader to get away from them now! You know with a perfect knowledge the song is a musical onion and will become a
part of you just as the carmeled onions became a part of my
students.

If the lyrics, along with the music, are uplifting or not contrary to Christ and his teachings, go for it! I hope you enjoy
these songs.

2. *Music.* The next major question when choosing music or
other forms of entertainment deals with the music itself. What
if the words are positive, inspiring, and uplifting, but the music
itself affects you in a negative way? What if it makes you feel
depressed, angry, violent, carnal, devilish, sensual, or any way
that is contrary to the teachings of Christ? Should we be listening to it? Is it harmless? Or can we listen to anything we want
and not be influenced in any way?

Can music in and of itself, regardless of lyrical content,
have an influence on the way we act, think, and feel? My research shows that music will generally do to a person what it

is written to do. It can excite. It can mellow. It can relax. It can agitate. It can lift spiritually. It can depress, and have many other profound influences upon us.

Music has always played a major role in my preparation for speaking, for spiritual communication, for athletic competitions, and in many other areas of my life. On most occasions it has accomplished the desired result. I must admit that I never did listen to the Tabernacle Choir before a big game, because it would do exactly what it was meant to do—get me in a spiritual frame of mind. Don't get me wrong; I always wanted to be spiritual, but playing in a major college football game was not the time to ask the linebacker across the line the "Golden Questions." Maybe after the game, but not during it. I would have been killed! However, I should quickly add that I never listened to "psyche" music appropriate for before games to prepare for a testimony meeting. Different types of music do cause different types of reactions and feelings. Therefore, if the music is persuading us "to do evil, and believe not in Christ, and deny him, and serve not God," then we know "with a perfect knowledge" it is inappropriate and should not be listened to (see Moroni 7:17).

Hopefully we have established the fact that music alone, without lyrical content, can have a profound influence on us. To illustrate this point, let us refer once again to television and movies. Even before movies had sound there was always an organ or a piano to create mood and to communicate feeling to the viewer. What would a movie be like without music? How would we ever know during a scary film that someone was hiding in the closet? How would we know when to be romantic, when to be nervous, when to be excited, when to cheer? If music were eliminated from movies I'm afraid moviegoers would seek out new forms of entertainment. Obviously it would simply be too boring to maintain our attention.

One of my favorite examples of music having a significant effect during a movie is the classic motion picture *Jaws*. If there had been no music during the opening scene, the movie would have lost its impact because the people viewing the picture would have had no idea what was going on. However, with the music, the entire story line is clear.

The movie begins with a young girl swimming near the beach. As she swims, she suddenly goes into jerking motions and has a look of terror on her face. Without music, the viewer wouldn't know if this young woman had stubbed her toe on the pier or hit her feet on the jagged coral below. By adding music to the scene, the viewer begins biting his fingernails, wincing with fear, curling up in his seat, or vocally screaming, "Get out! Get out!" Even without seeing anything the audience knows that a great white shark is about to attack the girl. With the music, when the girl's body goes into jerking motions the crowd moans with terror and vows never again to go swimming in the ocean.

Again, music will do what it is written to do. We, therefore, must be careful and judge wisely.

The producer, performer, and arranger all have certain objectives that they wish to achieve, whether it be to stimulate, depress, agitate, inspire, or uplift. However, we must remember that the name of the game in the music industry, or any media industry for that matter, is to make money. It is a business, and that which is going to increase revenues, good or bad, is that which is going to be sold and produced not only in America but everywhere. It has always been thus. Money will determine what music is produced. Money talks.

In their pursuit of material wealth and fame, many have lost their way. They have been blinded by the subtle craftiness of men who lie in wait to deceive. Their greed glands get stuck. They begin to serve a god other than our Father in Heaven, and sometimes do it innocently, not even realizing what is taking place. Thus, a large amount of the media is not edifying nor uplifting but is degrading and is leading us in a negative direction. It is often easy to take a low standard of morality, because it sells.

This idea of lowering standards in order to achieve wealth and money is not new. It has been going on since the beginning of time. The Savior taught the Nephites in 3 Nephi 27:32 that "they will sell me for silver and for gold, and for that which moth doth corrupt and which thieves can break through and steal."

Cain sold himself for his brother's flocks (see Moses 5:8–33). Judas Iscariot sold himself and our Master for thirty pieces of silver (see Matthew 26:14–16). The ancient Israelites were no different. They were worshipping false gods and selling themselves to do evil in the sight of the Lord: "And they left all the commandments of the Lord their God, and made them molten images, even two calves, and made a grove, and worshipped all the host of heaven, and served Baal. And they caused their sons and their daughters to pass through the fire, and used divination and enchantments, and sold themselves to do evil in the sight of the Lord, to provoke him to anger." (2 Kings 17:16–17.)

The Nephites also fell prey to this plague of seeking after that which is of no lasting importance and became involved with Satan and his counterfeits. After approximately two hundred years of perfect peace and harmony they became proud and thus fell into Satan's trap. Mormon wrote:

> And it came to pass that there were sorceries, and witchcrafts, and magics; and the power of the evil one was wrought upon all the face of the land, even unto the fulfilling of all the words of Abinadi, and also Samuel the Lamanite. . . .
>
> And it came to pass that the Nephites began to repent of their iniquity, and began to cry even as had been prophesied by Samuel the prophet; for behold no man could keep that which was his own, for the thieves, and the robbers, and the murderers, and the magic art, and the witchcraft which was in the land. (Mormon 1:19; 2:10.)

Knowing what went on in ancient times, is it any wonder then that the same types of activities and secret societies continue in our day? Why are we so alarmed when we read in the daily newspaper about all of the secret combinations that are being brought to light? The adversary and his followers are still trying to destroy all that is good. "Wherefore, he maketh war with the saints of God, and encompasseth them round about" (D&C 76:29). Music is simply one of their major methods.

Are there connections between the occult and certain types of music? Are witchcraft and devil worship thriving in our society today? The answer is clear: yes. Some performers enter the realms of the occult for various reasons—money, power, the desire to succeed—and they will do anything it takes to get to the top. They actually sell themselves "to do evil in the sight of the Lord" (2 Kings 17:17) in hopes of achieving success, praise, and financial increase.

It isn't necessary to go into a lengthy discussion on these matters. By delving into the subjects of devil worship or the occult in detail, we sometimes increase interest in them. It would be akin to giving a lecture to young people on pornography and holding up pornographic pictures to illustrate what you are talking about. Sure, you would get your point across, and at the same time probably cause someone in the audience to investigate this type of material further. Curiosity would be aroused, and instead of keeping people away from such filth you would give them ideas that they very possibly had never thought of before. The dark side is far more powerful than most people can imagine. Elder Boyd K. Packer has given us this advice: "A warning: There is a dark side to spiritual things. In a moment of curiosity or reckless bravado some teenagers have been tempted to toy with Satan worship. Don't you ever do that! Don't associate with those who do! You have no idea of the danger! And there are other foolish games and activities that are on that dark side. Leave them alone!"[12] The answer is to learn the true doctrine as taught by the prophets and the scriptures. Again, Elder Packer taught that "true doctrine, understood, changes attitudes and behavior. The study of the doctrines of the gospel will improve behavior quicker than a study of behavior will improve behavior. *Preoccupation with unworthy behavior can lead to unworthy behavior.* That is why we stress so forcefully the study of the doctrines of the gospel."[13] The scriptures contain the true doctrine and are replete with information concerning the effects of secret societies.

Perhaps the wisest counsel of all on this entire matter came from the ancient prophet Alma as he turned over the sacred records to his son Helaman. "And now, my son, I command you that ye retain all their oaths, and their covenants, and their agreements in their secret abominations; yea, and all their signs and their wonders ye shall keep from this people, that they know them not, lest peradventure they should fall into darkness also and be destroyed" (Alma 37:27).

Now we return to the original second question. If the words are good but the music is bad, should we be involved with it? Or if the music is known to have negative subliminal messages or it persuades us to act, think, or feel contrary to the teachings of Christ, should we be listening to it? No. Remember that the music of the drug and the hard rock culture is where the prophets have said that most of the problem lies. Remember—as President Packer said, "The tempo, the sounds, and the lifestyle of those who perform it repel the Spirit."[14] However, I admonish each reader to seek for that which is virtuous, lovely, of good report, and praiseworthy in contemporary as well as classical music.

3. *CD and tape covers; names of musical groups.* Should we listen to that music contained on the CD or cassette tape if the covers are promoting immorality, drug abuse, or violence and destruction, or are covered with gross illustrations and signs of witchcraft, devil worship, or the occult? At first this may seem easy, but the answer is not that simple. Often young people argue, "But, Brother Christianson, I don't listen to the covers." I understand that and realize that the covers may have nothing to do with the music inside, and may just be a technique to promote sales. However, if the artist or composer is willing to do anything to sell it, that tells us something. Again I refer to Moroni 7 and the thirteenth article of faith. If a cover is contrary to the teachings of Christ, it's difficult to see that the music inside it could be appropriate. Remember, it is unwise to give specific details concerning the signs of devil worship and witchcraft. But if there are things on the covers that are bla-

tantly in opposition to the teachings of Christ, we need to understand that there could be problems on the inside.

One day while walking through a local music store I had an experience that has been difficult to forget. I was interested in finding a particular piece of music that many of my students had purchased. While scanning the selections, my eyes caught a glimpse of a startling cover. The title was *Mob Rules*. There were some figures dressed in robes, with hoods over their faceless heads. Between them was a piece of canvas streaked with red paint. When I observed more closely, I realized that the streaks of red paint were not just streaks but a picture of Satan. As I recognized the face, which was the central figure of the picture, I realized why the figures had no faces. When a mob rules, individuality flees. I was then sickened by the thought that it was a mob that took Jesus and crucified him at Golgotha. It was a mob that murdered the Prophet Joseph Smith. It was an uncontrolled mob that caused the Mountain Meadow Massacre. I quickly put the music down and left the store without finding what I was originally looking for. I was truly sickened to think that some of my students felt that *Mob Rules* was just a catchy title and nothing more. I am not picking on this particular group, but if the covers are not in accordance with the standards we try so diligently to live by, we know they do not measure up to our guideline in Moroni 7.

How would we feel if we had to give the prophet a ride in our car and we had an inappropriate tape or CD on the front seat or in the glove compartment and he happened to see it? Would we be embarrassed and want to hide some of our collection? If we wouldn't feel comfortable, that's a good indication that our music is inappropriate.

4. *Music videos.* A brief yet simple story can serve as a meaningful introduction to this powerful music medium. Many years ago, as a missionary, I had an experience in the dry desert of New Mexico that affected me deeply. My companion and I had to pick up several new missionaries from the airport and drive them to their various assignments. After a short

meeting, we took the new elders to our favorite eating establishment and then proceeded with the task before us. As we drove around the city that evening, I began to feel tired and nauseated. I shrugged it off as nothing serious.

That night, however, the ill feelings increased. As I tried to sleep, my stomach turned and my head was spinning. Beads of sweat soaked my body; then moments later I felt like I was at the North Pole, chills covering every inch of me. The illness was relentless. After several miserable trips to the bathroom and hours of hot flashes and chills, I resolved that life was no longer worth living. If God was going to take my life, this was the perfect time. With these overly dramatic thoughts, I pleaded with the heavens to release me from the bondage of my illness and let me leave this mortal existence.

Fortunately for me, my prayers weren't answered. The next day, after a priesthood blessing and some scientific investigation, I not only recovered but discovered that I had suffered from severe food poisoning. I don't recall a time in my life when I felt more sick. That spoiled food was devastating.

As I ponder the memories of that dreadful night, the question arises: Why do so many people feel they can continue a diet of spoiled spiritual food and never suffer spiritual ailments? As has already been stated, we are as much what we listen to and watch as we are what we eat. Just as the spoiled food made me want to die, so can a diet of smut affect our desire for spiritual existence. President Spencer W. Kimball stated, "Teach your children to avoid smut as the plague it is. As citizens, join in the fight against obscenity in your communities. Do not be lulled into inaction by the pornographic profiteers who say that to remove obscenity is to deny people the rights of free choice. Do not let them masquerade licentiousness as liberty. Precious souls are at stake—souls that are near and dear to each of us."[15] When each of us considers the precious souls at stake, our menu of listening and viewing material must be considered closely.

With programs such as Music Television (MTV), the twenty-four-hour cable music station, and other cable networks, which show pornographic programs on a regular basis, another issue must be addressed. If the video of a song promotes or portrays attitudes, behaviors, feelings, or lifestyles contrary to the teachings of Christ or his prophets, should we participate in viewing them, and will they truly affect our own actions, feelings, thoughts, and spirituality? Does pairing a captivating musical score with a video or movie make the program more powerful or add impact to its message? The answer is obvious! Again, if a thirty-second commercial can sell a box of cereal, can a three-minute video sell a lifestyle?

Turn on MTV any time when young people are present and you can be assured that most other activities will cease and soon the program will have a mesmerized audience drinking deeply from its pictures.

There is something about "seeing" the music that is captivating. Today's listeners spend countless hours viewing what past generations only listened to. With the visual images being broadcast simultaneously with the audio, the motives of the composer and performer are brought home with force and fervor. Nothing, as in times past, is left to the imagination of the listener. The intent of the song is acted out before our eyes in vivid detail and unforgettable fashion. After watching the video once or twice, the images are planted firmly in our minds and can be recalled quickly and in detail with the slightest stimulus.

This medium is really nothing new. News reporters have used the visual technique to strengthen their stories since the inception of the movie theater and television.

I vividly remember going to the movie house in my hometown and watching a newsreel before every major movie. Everything from war to horse racing was broadcast, because few people in those days had the luxury of in-home televisions. Believe it or not, I still remember the content of some of those flittering black and white newscasts.

Dan Rather, anchorman for the CBS Evening News, makes a great case for why newspaper readers should also watch TV newscasts: "If you read a good newspaper every day you're going to know most, if not all, of what's on the evening news and probably a lot more but you won't have seen it. I think there's a difference between reading about the war and seeing some of it."[16]

An article in *Time* magazine said, "Social workers are almost unanimous in sighting the influence of the popular media—television, rock music, videos, movies—in propelling the trend toward precocious sexuality. One survey has shown that in the course of a year the average viewer sees more than 9,000 scenes of suggested sexual intercourse or innuendo on prime-time TV."[17]

A disconcerting thought is that with such a barrage of sexuality the message being broadcast is that to be sophisticated we have to be sexually hip. We have to know what's really going on. One author states that we don't even buy toothpaste to clean our teeth anymore; we buy it to be sexually attractive or to make sure we have fresh-smelling breath when we have an encounter with someone of the opposite sex.

Many people in the music and video business have without question picked up on one of the hottest ways of selling known to man—letting people see the product before they buy. Unfortunately, many of the selling techniques center around pornography, violence, and occult activities. Why? Because it sells to the masses! We must not forget that the major purpose for music videos and music TV programs is not primarily to educate but to sell. Money is the name of the game, even if spiritual ill health results. In fact, a member of the band Mötley Crüe stated, "We're the American youth and youth is about sex, drugs, pizza and more sex. We're intellectuals on a crotch level. We're the guys in high school your parents warned you to stay away from. That's what we're like on stage and off. The kids won't buy albums from phonies." Another band member went on to say, "I know people who pray for us every day. They can't save us. We're gone."[18]

Can this barrage of sexually explicit material and violence fail to have a profound effect upon the rising generation? United States Senator Robert Byrd made this obversation: "If we in this nation continue to sow the images of murder, violence, drug abuse, . . . perversion, pornography and aberration before the eyes of millions . . . , year after year and day after day, we should not be surprised if the foundations of our society rot away as if from leprosy."[19]

Victor B. Cline, a clinical psychologist, professor at the University of Utah, and nationally regarded expert on pornography's influence on society, wrote a stirring article titled "Obscenity—How It Affects Us, How We Can Deal with It." In this article the problem of "seeing" what we are listening to is brought masterfully into focus. He states:

> The outside world truly has entered into our homes—into the family room, the kitchen, and the bedroom. The seriousness of the problem has prompted this examination of a sensitive and distasteful subject.
>
> The media have a great potential to teach, inspire, inform, and entertain, but they may also corrupt, degrade, and pervert. They have the power to influence profoundly for good or evil all aspects of our values and feelings, as well as our behavior. We *are* affected by what we choose to expose ourselves to.
>
> For example, I have a letter from a fourteen-year-old girl telling of the death of her ten-year-old brother by hanging. With naive innocence, he had imitated the scene of a mock hanging he had witnessed in an evening television movie. He thought he could escape death as the actor in the movie had. He didn't.
>
> As a clinical psychologist, I see examples almost daily of gracious and good people (all ages, both sexes) of exemplary upbringing who have become addicted to viewing violence. Many have also cultivated an appetite for voyeuristically viewing stimulating, sexually explicit scenes of multiple adulteries, rape, or the seduction of innocents—all in living color and accompanied by a memorable musical score.
>
> Evil is presented as attractive and good. Destructive behaviors are marketed as exciting and rewarding. Often humor is used to make pornography, rape, or the loss of innocence entertaining and palatable.

But what starts out as a spectator sport introduces into one's brain a vast library of antisocial fantasies. These have the potential, much research suggests, of eventually being acted out—to the destruction of the individual and others around him.

I have found that four things typically happen to some people who become immersed in erotic or pornographic material.

First, they become addicted. They get hooked on it and come back for more and more.

Second, their desire for it escalates. They soon need rougher and more explicit material to get the same kicks and excitement.

Third, they become desensitized to the abnormality of the behavior portrayed. In time, they accept and embrace what at first had shocked and offended them.

Fourth, eventually there is a tendency and temptation to act out what they have witnessed. Appetite has been whetted and conscience anesthetized . . .

Those who witness this porno-violence in commercial cinema, on cable television, or on a rented videocassette—and who allow their children to view it—in my judgment do great injury to themselves and their children. This exposure creates false images and feelings about men and women and sexuality and raises the possibility that the viewer may be conditioned into practicing sexual deviancy. For, as much evidence has suggested, all sexual deviations are *learned,* not inherited.[20]

No wonder many people are losing interest in spiritual matters. They spiritually feed themselves on a diet that is totally nonnutritious. They become as sick spiritually as I had become physically from my spoiled dinner. In fact, President Kimball stated that the poisoning that takes place from viewing unwholesome material is worse than partaking of poisonous food. He said, "Each person must keep himself clean and free from lusts. He must shun ugly, polluted thoughts and acts as he would an enemy. Pornography and erotic stories and pictures are worse than polluted food. Shun them."[21]

Let us fill our lives and minds with only the good that exists in this magnificent teaching tool of music videos and movies. If we do not stay away from those music videos or movies that portray violent, profane, or pornographic images, any one of us could end up like the man who wrote President Gordon B. Hinckley a tragic letter concerning his addictions because of his viewing habits. He wrote:

> I am a 35-year-old male and am a convert to the Church of more than ten years. For most of my adult life I have been addicted to pornography. I am ashamed to admit this. My addiction is as real as that of an alcoholic or a drug addict.
>
> I was first introduced to this material as a child. I was molested by an older male cousin and pornography was used to attract my interest. I am convinced that this exposure at an early age to sex and pornography is at the root of my addiction today. I think it is ironic that those who support the business of pornography say that it is a matter of freedom of expression. I have no freedom. I have lost my free agency because I have been unable to overcome this. It is a trap for me, and I can't seem to get out of it. Please, please, please, plead with the brethren of the Church to not only avoid but eliminate the sources of pornographic material in their lives. . . .
>
> Finally, President Hinckley, please pray for me and others in the Church who may be like me to have the courage and strength to overcome this terrible affliction.[22]

President Hinckley then commented on the letter:

> There is neither happiness nor peace to be gained from surrendering to the weakness of indulging in these things which degrade and destroy. When such material is on television, turn off the set. Stop being a boob in front of the tube. Avoid titillating videotapes as you would a foul disease. They are in the same category. Stay away from pornographic magazines and other destructive literature. There is too much of good to see, there is too much of wonderful reading to be experienced to waste time and destroy character and willpower in submitting to such destructive rot.[23]

The words of Charles Dickens's classic novel *A Tale of Two Cities* ring in our ears: "It was the best of times, it was the worst of times." We live during an era when more is available for our good and comfort than at any other time in the earth's history. However, as far as sin and corruption are concerned, we live in some of the worst of times. Yet if we can remember the moving words of Joshua when others seek to have us choose music or any other thing that is contrary to godliness, we will always have "the best of times." Joshua beseeched, "Choose you this day whom ye will serve; . . . but as for me and my house, we will serve the Lord" (Joshua 24:15).

Good luck in your fishing!

Watch yourselves, and your thoughts,
and your words, and your deeds.
—Mosiah 4:30

6

Music and Our Actions, Feelings, and Thoughts

While attending a concert performed by the Mormon Youth Choir and Symphony I had an insightful experience. The production was marvelous. The music was uplifting, edifying, and resounding. It left me with a wonderful feeling. However, I almost missed hearing the music because of those sitting near me.

Just to my right was a young man sitting with his mother, totally engrossed in the music. At times he would have to restrain himself from clapping during each musical number. At other times he was tapping his feet. Then, without any notice or warning, tears would roll down his cheeks as the symphony would play songs that touched his heart. I found myself entranced by the effect the music had upon him. Then my eyes caught an older gentleman sitting two rows in front of me. He was singing the words to himself and conducting the music as if he were in front of the stand, moving his hands in a 4/4 beat and then a 2/4 beat, matching the rhythm of the song being performed.

I could not help but say to myself, *And people say music*

doesn't have any effect upon the way we act, think, or feel? It was entertaining and educational not only to watch and listen to the symphony and choir but to watch the audience as well.

One of the most fascinating phenomena in the world is the manner in which music affects human thought, feeling, action, and spiritual awareness. As I travel, I never cease being amazed at how hairstyles, dress, speech, attitude, social behavior, recreational choices, and other activities are affected, each in its own way, by the music an individual devotes himself to, and by the heroes and heroines in that particular genre of music.

See for yourself. As you go to the store or to a ball game, observe how many of the styles you see had their beginning on a poster or album cover, in a popular movie, or in a music fad promoted by radio, video, or music television. Indeed, much of our modern environment is affected by music.

In a general conference address Elder Ezra Taft Benson quoted the late Richard Nibley, a former teacher of music at Snow College in Ephraim, Utah, who said, "Music creates atmosphere. Atmosphere creates environment. Environment influences behavior." Mr. Nibley had explained that the mechanics of the atmosphere-environment-behavior relationship are rhythm or beat, volume, repetition, gyrations, darkness, and flashing lights.[1]

Many consider rhythm to be the very heart of music because of its profound effect on the individual. Rhythm, a patterned measure of time, causes the natural tapping of the foot, the fingers, or a pencil as we listen. Small children are interesting to watch because of their total honesty and lack of inhibition. Without having been taught the intricacies of music, they instinctively begin to move in time with whatever music they happen to hear. It is rhythm or beat that causes such actions.

Richard Nibley explained this further, as quoted by Elder Benson: "Rhythm is the most physical element in music. It is the only element in music that can exist in bodily movement without benefit of sound. A mind dulled by drugs or alcohol can still respond to the beat."[2]

A behavioral kinesiologist, Dr. John Diamond, said, "With

the ears completely blocked, the body still responds to sound. This is because we 'hear' not only with our ears, but also with our bodies."[3]

Dr. Reid Nibley, former professor of music at Brigham Young University, discussed this remarkable power. In an interview he said that, according to two psychologists, music influenced the digestive, secretory, circulatory, nutritive and respiratory functions of the body. "Musical sounds can be so manipulated as to induce alternating states of tension and relaxation," he said. "The melody can affect the larynx involuntarily. As music goes higher, there is more tension; down brings more relaxation." He said that can affect the heart, skeletal muscles, and motor nerves, and that repeated patterns can cause light hypnosis.[4]

This potential for hypnosis is in harmony with the comment of two famous singers who quit the business when they realized what their music was doing to people. One asserted that the music he performed "clouds the senses and hypnotizes the brain. When you get people at their weakest point you can preach into the subconscious what you want to say."[5]

That idea is a little frightening. On this point, Dr. Reid Nibley continued, "Sustained chords lower blood pressure; crisp, repeated chords raise it. Loud volume stimulates responses of hormone secretion in addition to nervous and muscular tension."[6]

A fascinating study was conducted by Dr. Diamond and is recorded in his book *Your Body Doesn't Lie*. Dr. Diamond made an in-depth study of the function of the body. His discoveries are quite remarkable but very logical. His major thesis concerning music is that because of the heartbeat and the rhythm of the music, our bodies are profoundly affected. The "da da dah, da da dah" beat, known in poetry as the anapestic beat, is common in many rock records. However, its effect appears to be different when used with music than when used in poetry. "The rock beat appears to be addictive; repeated exposure to it causes one to seek it. It becomes the beat of choice."[7] He goes on to say that our bodies are physically affected and our muscles are weakened by this particular beat. It is almost impossible for the muscle to have full strength while listening to the anapestic beat. On the other hand, many muscles are strengthened with other types of beats and rhythms.

He does mention that not all rock numbers have this weakening effect, nor does any particular group necessarily have the effect consistently. He mentions that earlier rock 'n' roll songs did not have the effect that the hard rock music of today does. He tested over twenty thousand records of all types of music and found that the only type of music other than hard rock that caused the muscles to go weak was a short segment of Haitian voodoo drumming.

In classical music he found only two instances that produced muscle weakness. One was at the conclusion of Stravinsky's *Rite of Spring* and the other at the conclusion of Ravel's *La Valse*. In both instances the composer was attempting to convey chaos, which he obviously did quite successfully.[8]

According to Dr. Diamond, not only is this particular rock beat addictive, as mentioned before, and not only does repeated exposure cause one to seek it, but it throws the entire body into a state of alarm. It causes major changes to occur in children. Their performance in school decreases and hyperactivity and restlessness increase.[9]

In adults, Dr. Diamond found a decreased work output, increased errors, general inefficiency, reduced decision-making capacity on the job, and a nagging feeling that things just weren't right. He goes on to say that the major problem he saw was a loss of energy for no apparent reason. He also found that the academic records of many schoolchildren improved considerably after they stopped listening to rock music while studying.[10]

More recently Drs. Frances Rauscher and Gordon Shaw of the University of California-Irvine have done research that supports some of Dr. Diamond's conclusions. They found that having children take music lessons, encouraging them to enjoy music, and perhaps playing Mozart concertos for them can significantly enhance their ability to learn. Dr. Rauscher suggests that by having children take music lessons as early as possible, parents may be able to improve "reasoning abilities . . . crucial for such higher brain functions as music, complex mathematics and chess." They suggest that music programs in schools should never be eliminated or cut financially.

> Rauscher said it's not known what type of music is best for children as far as improving their intellectual capabilities, but "the more complex, apparently the better."
>
> In other words, she said, children apparently are better off listening to or trying to play Mozart than they would be spending their time on rock music with repetitive lyrics and jingles.
>
> Even having your kids listen to music apparently will improve their intellectual capabilities, she said, but actually learning how to read and play music seems to have a much more dramatic effect.[11]

In studies conducted at New York University the playing of certain types of music was found to inspire many people to score better on various mental tests than they did without the influence of music. Then at Louisiana State University investigators compared the performance of students who took mental tests while listening to classical, jazz, rock 'n' roll, or no music. Students received the lowest scores on the tests when rock 'n' roll was played.[12]

When it comes to learning and music and retaining information, Dr. Georgie Losinov, a leading psychiatrist from Sophia, Bulgaria, has done a tremendous amount of work on this subject, and the results of much of his research are recorded in a book titled *Super Learning*. Dr. Losinov developed a method of cue-reinforced learning that is sometimes known as suggestology or suggestopedic learning. It involves rhythmic or repeated listening using music as a relaxation technique to help people rapidly learn things such as foreign languages and lists of factual data. The results of his research are stunning to many educators because they reveal a person's ability to learn when using the powerful force of music, along with other scientific methods.[13]

Once again, I'm not on a crusade against any type of music, but it seems obvious that if certain types of music, particularly hard rock, have such a negative effect on learning, we should be wise and not digest such material.

A number of studies have been conducted at universities across the country concerning the effects of music on the physical body. For example, the behavior of unruly and hyperactive children is markedly improved by playing background music. Popular children's records being played result in marked improvement in children's behavior. Also, by such procedures productivity of hyperactive children in a schoolroom setting is enhanced.[14]

It has also been found that unborn children are profoundly affected by the music their mother is exposed to. Children who are read or talked to or have good music stimulation while in the womb have been found to react to sound and vocal stimuli better than those who have not received such stimulation. They are also found to be soothed much more easily when music is played.[15]

Music has a profound effect on us even while driving in stressful traffic. It has been found that the chance of an accident is reduced when the car radio is on. I know this sounds crazy, but institutional studies have shown that music played at peak accident periods has resulted in a lower accident rate because the music can offset the effect of nerve-sapping tensions and aggressive driver reactions, which often build up during these stressful time periods. Some music (mood, instrumental, choir, and semi-classical) has even increased the production of mothers' milk while nursing by as much as 50 to 150 percent.[16]

Does music have an effect on our bodies and our actions? Of course it does. Therefore, we must listen to only that which is going to have a positive effect upon us.

What about our thoughts and feelings? Are they as profoundly affected by the music we listen to as are our actions? The evidence again is overwhelmingly yes. Tolstoy said,

"Music makes me forget my real situation. It transports me into a state which is not my own. Under the influence of music I really seem to feel what I do not understand, to have powers which I cannot have."[17]

In chapter 2 we discussed what a profound influence music has on our everyday lives. Most of us go about our lives having no real thought of how the music we listen to, the videos we see, or the words we sing affect our minds and feelings. Could we be much more careful about what we let filter through our minds? Alma taught, "For our words will condemn us, yea, all our works will condemn us; we shall not be found spotless; and our thoughts will also condemn us" (Alma 12:14). Remember, we are, or will become, what we think about most of the time. It becomes as much a part of our lives as the onions became a part of my student.

Napoleon Hill, in his classic book *Think and Grow Rich,* said, "Our brains become magnetized with the dominating thoughts which we hold in our minds. And by means with which no man is familiar, these magnets attract to us the forces, the people, and circumstances of life which harmonize with the nature of our dominating thoughts."[18] The lyrics, the words, the scenes from the videos constantly flowing through our minds cannot help but have a profound effect on what we think and how we feel.

As was also discussed earlier, we can in reality forget nothing. Every experience, every word becomes a part of our lives and our being. In recent years this idea has been demonstrated by world authorities during brain surgery. Drs. Penfield and Roberts of the Montreal Neurological Institute have literally confirmed that we don't forget anything. It all is stored in our brains. It is just a simple matter of recall, not of remembering or forgetting but of bringing it back. During brain surgery when they stimulated certain brain cells with an electrode, the patients on whom they were working reported the sensation of reliving scenes from their past. Their recall was so vivid that all details were present including sounds, colors, and odors.[19]

Where does music fit in all of this? In addition to music

being one of the greatest ways that we have to learn things, it also has other positive effects. When people become depressed, psychological studies show that they often resist strenuous verbal efforts to cheer them up. But investigators at a leading university found that depressed subjects responded favorably to lively, exciting music, because it affects people on a feeling rather than a thinking level.[20]

When a young person becomes angry in the home, what does he or she do? Although this isn't always the case, it has been my experience that many young people retreat to their rooms and crank up the music as loud as possible. Why? Because the music "harmonizes" with the feelings they feel. We usually want to listen to music that agrees with how we want to feel about ourselves, others, or current circumstances. Selecting music that coincides with a person's actual mood is known by psychologists as the iso-principle. When using the iso-principle for a person who is depressed, downbeat music is matched to the depressed mood. Then, by stages, the music is changed to more upbeat music, thereby altering the mood of the subject. As one investigator pointed out, matching the mood of the music to the mood of the person is necessary because otherwise the subject will reject the music. But by degrees we can shift the music and carry the subject's mood into a more tranquil state.[21]

Does this little bit of information answer questions as to why so many people today are angry with society, with the world, with themselves? Take a look at the music they listen to. What videos are they watching? Are they filled with violence, anger, or both? Have we found violence to be the cure to all of society's woes? President Thomas S. Monson quoted an article from the *Deseret News* that contained this observation: "A society that views graphic violence as entertainment . . . should not be surprised when senseless violence shatters the dreams of its youngest and brightest."[22] Our feelings and thoughts can many times reflect the type of music or other forms of entertainment we listen to or watch.

President Spencer W. Kimball commented on the close relationship between the instruments played and the feelings they induce:

> Musical sounds can be put together in such a way that they can express feelings—from the most profoundly exalted to the most abjectly vulgar. Or rather, these musical sounds induce in the listener feelings which he responds to, and the response he makes to these sounds has been called a "gesture of the spirit." Thus, music can act upon our senses to produce or induce feelings of reverence, humility, fervor, assurance, or other feelings attuned to the spirit of worship. When music is performed in Church which conveys a "gesture" other than that which is associated with worship, we are disturbed . . . to the degree with which the musical "gesture" departs from or conflicts with the appropriate representation of feelings of worship.[23]

As far as our thoughts are concerned, most of us struggle at one time or another to keep them clean and pure. In today's world it is difficult to blot from our perceptions all the vulgar and profane material the world puts before us. If, however, we provide a place for our thoughts to go, we can control them. They need not control us. The old adage applies: "You can't keep birds from flying over your head, but you can keep them from making a nest in your hair." We may not always be able to control what flits into our minds, but we can control how long it stays there.

Without virtuous thoughts, it is easy to find ourselves lacking in confidence, in having the Holy Ghost as our constant companion, and in having the doctrine of the priesthood distil upon our souls (see D&C 121:45–46).

I especially like what Elder Boyd K. Packer has said about music and our thoughts:

> Probably the greatest challenge to people of any age, particularly young people, and the most difficult thing you will face in mortal life is to learn to control your thoughts. As a

man "thinketh in his heart, so is he." (Proverbs 23:7.) One who can control his thoughts has conquered himself. . . .

I want to tell you young people about one way you can learn to control your thoughts, and it has to do with music.

The mind is like a stage. Except when we are asleep the curtain is always up. There is always some act being performed on that stage. It may be a comedy, a tragedy, interesting or dull, good or bad; but always there is some act playing on the stage of the mind. . . .

If you can control your thoughts, you can overcome habits, even degrading personal habits. If you can learn to master them you will have a happy life.

This is what I would teach you. Choose from among the sacred music of the Church a favorite hymn, one with words that are uplifting and music that is reverent, one that makes you feel something akin to inspiration. Remember President Lee's counsel; perhaps "I Am a Child of God" would do. Go over it in your mind carefully. Memorize it. Even though you have had no musical training, you can think through a hymn.

Now, use this hymn as the place for your thoughts to go. Make it your emergency channel. Whenever you find these shady actors have slipped from the sidelines of your thinking onto the stage of your mind, put on this record, as it were.

As the music begins and as the words form in your thoughts, the unworthy ones will slip shamefully away. It will change the whole mood on the stage of your mind. Because it is uplifting and clean, the baser thoughts will disappear. For while virtue, by choice, *will not* associate with filth, evil *cannot* tolerate the presence of light.

In due time you will find yourself, on occasion, humming the music inwardly.[24]

This formula certainly works for me. My hymns are "I Know That My Redeemer Lives," "Because I Have Been Given Much," and "I Believe in Christ." I sing them when inappropriate thoughts try to enter my mind. Over the years my mind has become much like a stereo system that goes to automatic, and as the music begins to play, the evil thought departs.

Elder Packer continued,

> Once you learn to clear the stage of your mind from unworthy thoughts, keep it busy with learning worthwhile things. Change your environment so that you have things about you that will inspire good and uplifting thoughts. Keep busy with things that are righteous.
>
> Young people, you cannot afford to fill your mind with the unworthy hard music of our day. It is *not* harmless. It can welcome onto the stage of your mind unworthy thoughts and set the tempo to which they dance and to which you may act.
>
> You degrade yourself when you identify with all of those things which seem now to surround such extremes in music: the shabbiness, the irreverence, the immorality, and the addictions. Such music as that is not worthy of you. You should have self-respect.
>
> You are a son or a daughter of Almighty God. He has inspired a world full of wonderful things to learn and to do, uplifting music of many kinds that you may enjoy.[25]

Human beings are not the only creations of God that are drastically affected by various types of music. Plants and various animals are also. Moses 3:5 tells us, "For I, the Lord God, created all things, of which I have spoken, spiritually, before they were naturally upon the face of the earth." If all things were created spiritually, which they were, then the old adage "Music hath charms to soothe the savage beast" may well apply in the animal and plant kingdom.

The reader may enjoy and be interested in a few experiments that were performed concerning plants and animals and how they responded to various types of music. These experiments may sound a little crazy. But if all things were created spiritually before they were created temporally, it seems logical that they would respond differently to that which is of God and that which is not.

The first involves a Tulsa, Oklahoma, radio station that dedicated soft, mellow songs to the cows each morning because they were so touchy around milking time. The music soothed these animals and they produced better milk. Gene Neill of Associated Milk Producers also said that acid rock almost dried the cows up.[26]

The second experiment deals with a young girl from Ogden, Utah, who used her sagebrush lizard and her northeastern fence lizard. The lizards were exposed to various types of music for ten days. She entered her experiment in the 1981 Weber Regional Science Fair, and her findings were later reported in the *Ogden Standard Examiner.*

> For the first few days she played classical music—mostly symphonies, but some instrumental arrangements of hymns. The lizards responded ecstatically to the serious music.
>
> They climbed up on the rocks to get closer to the speakers. They lifted their faces up to the source of the music.
>
> The report indicated that they also grew during their classical concerts. Each of them gained about a gram.
>
> The next series of music the lizards were subjected to was country western. They lost their uplift and paced back and forth across the terrarium, acting as if they were ornery with each other. They also lost half a gram in weight.
>
> The final series of music was hard rock. During this concert they lost another half a gram apiece and buried themselves in the sand, even to the point of hiding their heads.[27]

At this time there is no way of judging the validity of this girl's findings, but her results are very interesting.

Dr. Reid Nibley reported to the BYU student body a third set of experiments. His source was an article in the *Denver Post.*

> A series of experiments conducted for nearly two years by Mrs. Dorothy Retallack of Denver showed that assorted plants have been killed by exposing them to rock music.
>
> She discovered that just three hours of acid rock a day

shrivels young squash plants and flattens philodendrons and crumbles corn in less than a month.

Mrs. Retallack piped to her plants—placed in controlled environment chambers—music from two Denver radio stations. One group of plants was exposed to a rock station and another group to a semi-classical station.

The results: "The petunias listening to rock refused to bloom. Those on classical developed six beautiful blooms. By the end of the second week, the 'rock' petunias were leaning away from the radio and showing very erratic growth. The 'classical' petunias were all leaning toward the sound. Within a month all plants exposed to rock music died."[28]

Mrs. Retallack conducted further experiments on various groups and types of vegetable plants with similar results.

These experiments are cited only as points of interest—and they are interesting. On reading of such experiments, I wonder just how much influence some of our popular music today is having not only on individual lives but on our entire environment.

Because of my interest in this aspect of music, I find it immensely enjoyable to expose those to whom I speak to a variety of music. (Of course, I am careful in the pieces I select—as you should be too, if you decide to try an experiment of your own.) In spite of the good times the audiences and I often have, there are always a few people who, for some reason, are reluctant to admit the effects of music on them until they are actually challenged in a learning-by-doing situation.

I like to start by tuning in stations up and down the FM radio dial. The reactions of young and old alike are hilarious as they hear the songs they either adore or despise.

A good station to start with is an "elevator music" station. It is also the kind of music you would hear in the dentist's chair or the supermarket. Many parents smile when they hear it, but most of the young generation plead with me to turn it off. When asked what the station is, most of them know the correct answer. "How come you know it if you never listen to it?" I ask them. Invariably someone responds, "It reminds me of my mother," a classic admission that music does affect our feelings.

Next I move to some country western music. People start clapping and hee-hawing, preparing to mount an imaginary horse and ride off into the sunset.

As I go through various selections of music, I watch forehead movement and facial expression. I hear whispered conversations stimulated by what is heard. It is indeed quite a show.

Inevitably when I play a current popular tune, or one that was popular ten to thirty years ago, I see a young girl or older woman begin to blush. You know the rest. She nudges a neighbor or her husband with her elbow and says, "Why, that's our song." Music stimulates memories, and listeners have to share them.

Sometimes I have played the themes from the various *Rocky* movies. Unless you see this experiment or try it yourself, it's hard to believe what happens. People take deep breaths and bulge their chests out as if they could conquer the world. Heads begin to jerk with the beat, hands are raised above the head in clenched fists, and some people start punching their neighbors like a punching bag. I don't have to tell people what the titles are; they respond to feelings that stir inside them.

Sometimes it is difficult to control myself. I picture in my mind's eye a drill team at a football game during halftime, and I even feel an impulse to act accordingly. My arms fly out in front of me, my head moves from side to side, and my legs want to march. I doubt if I would ever behave like that without the aid of that tune.

After the audience sees how much their thoughts, feelings, and actions are influenced by the music they hear, the entire mood of the meeting is changed by playing songs by the Mormon Tabernacle Choir or a soft, peaceful piece with a background of rolling waves and faint seagull cries. There is a metamorphosis in the audience. Suddenly a vibrant, excited group becomes calm, sleepy, and docile.

People are eager to express what they feel and think in that peaceful minute. I enjoy their responses because they are basically all the same. They recite the scenes that were implanted in their minds by the music. After the spirit of the meeting has been set by the peaceful music, we are ready to discuss the effects of music on our spirits.

It is not by chance that you have been reserved to come
to earth in this last dispensation of the fulness of times.
Your birth at this particular time was
foreordained in the eternities.
—*Ezra Taft Benson*

7

Listening to a Prophet's Voice

Many years ago I taught a couple of classes that were particularly difficult to handle. Some students would trail into class with little interest in learning anything, especially about the Savior or the scriptures that taught about him. I was troubled. Often I would go home discouraged, wanting to leave the teaching profession. It seemed as if very few students were being affected. I felt that I was wasting my time. Then one day after class a student brought me a popular album and asked me to listen to the words of a song it contained.

We went into my office and played the song, listening closely to the music as well as the lyrics. The music was depressing. It made me feel like I was being chased by some creature of the unknown through a graveyard at night in the fog. It was so depressing that I wanted to stop the music. But the student insisted my hearing the words. He felt I would be interested in their message. I have never been able to forget what I heard that afternoon:

> Well, I don't want no preacher telling me about a God
>   in the sky.
> No, I don't want no one telling me where I'm gonna go
>   when I die.
> I'm gonna live my life, don't want people telling me
>   what to do.
> I'll just believe in myself 'cause no one else is true.

These words, coupled with music that would go well in a horror movie, were not the worst lyrics I had heard but were preaching some of the greatest false doctrine ever taught: namely, that a person need not worry about God nor what happens after death, and that an individual is just that—an individual, with no need for others. He must live his own life, depending on no one. Could this be one of the reasons so many of my students seemed so disinterested?

More recently I have had many other experiences, too numerous to mention, that have verified some of the feelings of years past as to why so many people, young and old alike, have little interest in spiritual things. I would like to briefly relate just two of these. The first is from a young man who attended a Metallica concert just days before entering the mission field. He shared with me, by way of letter, his journal entry from 2:00 A.M. the morning after the concert.

> I have just returned from seeing Metallica in concert. This has marked the final major "evil" in my life. I have been overwhelmed by the Spirit the last couple of days and have been experiencing it for several months now, and what took place at the concert was utterly demoralizing. I watched 20,000 people cheer on Metallica. I watched 20,000 cheer on Salt Lake City as they showed the street sign on one of the television monitors. I watched 20,000 cheer with the most crude and foul language ever used by man, with the tone of violence in their every yell. I watched them all then boo the "This Is the Place" monument as it appeared on-screen. I then

watched, which shattered my spirits the worst, 20,000 people—children of God—boo and flip off the Salt Lake City temple of the Lord. How evil this was to see, and worst of all, it actually hurt inside to see it. This had never affected me this way before. I had such a hard time at the concert. Never, hardly for a moment, did the knowledge of the gospel, our purpose here on this earth, and the recent experiences with it leave my mind. I made the comparisons of good and evil over and over throughout the concert and how some of these people could overcome the evilness of what was transpiring. . . .

Right now it is 2:00 A.M. I feel a sense of a lost spirit because until lately I'd never experienced the great amount of love and the great feelings of the good. This is why these people are this way. The good is made out to be the bad, and so the evil is made out to be the good. . . .

I truly felt as though Satan was hovering over the center of the stage, his legs folded in a sitting position and his right hand under his chin, just laughing with the most hideous, indescribable laughter in the world, saying, "Look at all my followers and all the evil I have accomplished. Look at all them, how stupid they all are to fall so easily—no one will return to Christ."

I honestly felt that at this point in the concert I actually saw him there off and on.

All these people have some good in them—the desire to smile, love, and help each other. But as the concert progressed I saw that leave all of them. The hate filled all, the adrenaline filled people, yelling, screaming, swearing, hating, waiting to unleash all their adrenaline in some other way, quicker and more aggressive. All one saw in their eyes was hate and evil. I saw people not worshipping Satan but Metallica and evil, which are products of Satan, not Christ.

This young man continued for page after page, describing the blackness, the immodesty, the drinking, the smoking, the yelling, the screaming, the swearing, the fighting, and the drugs. He concludes:

I never knew it this way before in my life. . . . This is a feeling that is a product of a degenerating or deteriorating spirit, and this path speeds the process so fast and will take it to a point of no return in a short time. It is that feeling attained when one loses any sense of what he wants and needs and what life is truly about. I feel so strong that once one lets the true meaning of life out of his grasp, all is lost. Not always as easy as that, but generally like that.

Keep in mind, I've shared only a very small part of the journal entry. But as I read it in its entirety, it is not hard to see why the worshippers of Metallica would not desire spiritual food.

The second experience also occurred in Salt Lake City at a Nine Inch Nails concert. Marilyn Manson, the opening act for Nine Inch Nails, was not allowed to perform in Salt Lake City because of the offensive content of his musical material. In protest, before Nine Inch Nails began their concert Manson came onto the stage, ripped up a copy of the Book of Mormon, and threw it into the audience, saying, "Do you let him [meaning God] run your lives?"[1]

Could those who witnessed this scene of destruction of "the most correct of any book on earth"[2] be desensitized to the promptings of the Spirit?

If a person young or old has a constant diet of such music, how is he or she likely to respond when parents, teachers, or friends admonish, "Gather round; today I would like to teach you about God in the sky. Today I would really like to discuss where you go when you die."

Not all people would respond the same way. But knowing what we know about music, if a person never listened to much else, what would his reactions likely be? Would spiritual matters lose their importance? Would statements such as "You can't tell me what to do," or "It's my life, and if I want to throw it away it's none of your business," or "Just leave me alone!" become the norm?

When considering such questions and this experience with my student years ago, my heart aches. Is it really an individual's life? Does a person have the right to mess it up or live it any way he or she chooses? Though we may have the agency to choose for ourselves, it is vital to remember that we are responsible and accountable for our choices (see Revelation 20:12–13). As the old saying goes, you can't pick up one end of the stick without picking up the other.

Nearly two thousand years ago the greatest blood that ever coursed through veins was spilt on the ground of a dusty garden and on a cross so that you and I could be forgiven of our sins and live forever. To put it simply, the greatest sacrifice in the history of this universe, and the highest price ever paid for anything, were given for you and me. Through the atoning sacrifice of Jesus Christ we were each bought for a price, the price being the life of the Son of God.

Yes, we were bought. The price paid was so high that most of us have but a faint notion of its significance. The Apostle Paul taught us well on this subject: "What? know ye not that your body is the temple of the Holy Ghost which is in you, which ye have of God, and ye are not your own? For ye are bought with a price: therefore glorify God in your body, and in your spirit, which are God's." (1 Corinthians 6:19–20.)

When considering this ultimate act of love, my heartstrings are wrenched with pain, yet my eyes cry tears of joy. My soul sings out the words, "Oh, it is wonderful that he should care for me enough to die for me!"[3]

Why did he pay such a price? Why do we oftentimes, along with the world, appear to reject his ultimate sacrifice? Perhaps the words of the prophet Nephi answer these two questions best: "And the world, because of their iniquity, shall judge him to be a thing of naught; wherefore they scourge him, and he suffereth it; and they smite him, and he suffereth it. Yea, they spit upon him, and he suffereth it, because of his loving kindness and his long-suffering towards the children of men." (1 Nephi 19:9.)

Let us not think of this price as a "thing of naught." Let us not "trample under [our] feet the Holy One" (see Helaman 12:2).

Now let us refer back to the words of the song at the beginning of this chapter. After contemplating such a heavy topic as the atonement of Christ, can you see why Satan, with his various methods, would try to get people to believe that it is unimportant to learn about "God in the sky" or where you are going when you die? To me, it appears obvious that if he can deceive us into believing false doctrine, it can have a catastrophic effect on our spirituality.

Heber J. Grant said, "The more beautiful the music by which false doctrine is sung, the more dangerous it becomes."[4]

This is where I find the thickest walls of resistance as I speak on this subject. Many understand that much of the music they listen to is not so good, but they honestly believe that it will not affect their spirituality.

"They're just kids, for heaven's sake. Let them have their fun. They'll grow out of it." These statements are commonly heard from some parents and leaders. Or some have commented, "Our kids would never let their music affect them adversely. Besides, some of the music isn't that bad, is it?" Some even contend, "If we don't allow them to listen to it, they'll just go somewhere else to get it."

I cringe when I hear songs promoting immorality, drug abuse, or rebellion being played at church functions simply because that is the only way we can get some of our youth to come to the activities. President J. Reuben Clark commented concerning such philosophies, "We may not, under our duty, provide or tolerate an unwholesome amusement on the theory that if we do not provide it the youth will go elsewhere to get it. We could hardly set up a roulette table in the Church amusement hall for gambling purposes, with the excuse that if we do not provide it the youth would go to a gambling hall to gamble. We can never really hold our youth thus. Our task is to help the home to plant better standards in the minds of the youth."[5]

We cannot have the attitude that it will go away or that the problem is everywhere else but in our home or our valley. One of Satan's greatest traps is to lead us into believing that there is no problem, or that whatever the problem is, "It will never affect me or mine," or that "I'm different from everyone else."

When I hear statements such as these and I see people believing that music will not affect their spirit, 2 Nephi 28:21 comes to mind. "And others will he [Satan] pacify, and lull them away into carnal security, that they will say: All is well in Zion; yea, Zion prospereth, all is well—and thus the devil cheateth their souls, and leadeth them away carefully down to hell."

When we get the attitude that our music, or any other thing, will never affect us, then we are ripe to be led "carefully down to hell." A short story about fishing on the Provo River illustrates this scripture wonderfully.

I have learned that if you want to catch the small ones, it is not that difficult. You don't have to be very careful. Simply follow a few basic procedures, and nearly every time you go fishing you can catch one or two. However, catching the big German Brown is a different story altogether. Being careful and patient are vital for success.

When I was a younger man I loved to put a fly or spinner on my line and work a few secret spots on the river, waiting for that "big one" to take what I offered. I always knew he was under there, watching my fly hit and skim across the water time after time, and I'd wonder if he dared to take it. He'd look, swim a little closer, and seem to say, "I know it's probably from a local sporting goods store, but it looks so good I've got to have it!" I'd tease him more by working the fly back and forth until finally he would think, "I know it's not good, but I've handled it before; I'm sure I can handle it again." Then, *boom!* He would hit it hard and start to swim vigorously upstream. I'd let out a lot of line and let him think that he had gotten away with it. Then, when he felt that he had succeeded, I would carefully, very carefully, reel him in. He would still appear to be swimming so well that it would be difficult for him to believe he was in any danger.

Suddenly he'd see my green boots. Reality would strike, and he'd groan, "Oh no, if my parents knew I were here, they'd kill me!" With that statement he would fight harder than ever before. He'd know he was in trouble. I had him right where I wanted him. I would continue to keep pressure on my line as I raised my pole above my head. With my free hand I would reach for my net and carefully lower it under his fighting body.

The fish, knowing he was in trouble, would fight diligently, but by then his efforts would be meaningless. Once he was in my net, I'd secure my pole beneath my arm and grab the fish carefully with one hand. I'd dislodge the fly, hold the fish up, and say, "You really thought it was good, didn't you! Sorry!" I then would open my pouch, put him in it, and go on trying to catch another. He, on the other hand, would hardly know what had happened. He'd wonder, as he looks out of the small hole in my pouch, *How could this ever happen to me? This doesn't happen in real life. It only happens on soap operas!* He had been caught, having been led carefully into my trap.

Are we sometimes like the fish with our music or videos? Satan can catch many people with little effort, just as I could catch the small fish. But when he goes after one who has been taught truth, he must be much more careful.

Are we being led away with our entertainment so carefully by the master deceiver that we don't even know it is happening? Does some of the music of our day appear to be so good that we are being reeled in hook, line, and sinker? Elder Ezra Taft Benson said, "Rock music, with its instant physical appeal, is an ideal doorcrasher, for the devil knows that music has the power to ennoble or corrupt, to purify or pollute. He will not forget to use its subtle power against you."[6]

Satan's music often looks so good that we may begin to believe that we cannot resist; we feel it is having little or no effect on us until he lowers the net, raises us up, and inserts his fingers through our spiritual gills. He then opens his pouch, drops us in, and closes the lid. As we, like the fish, gaze out of the small hole, we finally realize that we are in trouble, that we have been deceived. Alma's words referring to Korihor, the anti-Christ, ring loudly in our ears: "And thus we see the end of him who perverteth the ways of the Lord; and thus we see that the devil will not support his children at the last day, but doth speedily drag them down to hell" (Alma 30:60).

As we lie there, we begin wondering how our lives became so misled in such a short period of time. We should be thankful to God that the price was paid. We are better off by far than the fish, for we have a loving Father who provided a way for us to change our course and rechart our lives, if we will but accept it.

Unfortunately there are those who sink so low because of their inappropriate choices that they never do get out of Satan's trap. While speaking at a leadership seminar for high school student leaders and their advisers and guidance counselors I had a sobering experience. After the speech was over several people asked some specific questions about music and current popular artists. One question came from a guidance counselor at a local high school. He asked, "Have you been following the murder trial for _____ (let's call him Bill) on the local news?" I indicated that I had because the young man being tried for murder was a former student of one of my teaching colleagues. The young man had called my colleague from jail and asked him to come and talk with him shortly after his arrest. The murder had made headlines in most major papers around the country. As the trial progressed, the local media reported on the story almost every day. All of us standing there in the room knew what the counselor was talking about.

"Well," he continued, "I was his high school guidance counselor. Shortly after his arrest I met with him in jail. We talked for some time about the entire situation. I then asked him a penetrating question.

"'Bill, how did someone like you from a strong Latter-day Saint family, with good upbringing, go from being active in school and your teachers quorum to skipping school, forsaking church, to drug addiction, to devil worship, to murder? How did your life take such a tragic turn in just three years?'"

Bill's unhesitating answer to the counselor surprised even me. I don't know what I expected, but his answer floored me.

"My music," he had said. The counselor then went on quoting Bill.

"'I wanted to be just like my heroes I was listening to. They sang of death, drugs, violence, sex, and the occult. I wanted to know what it was like.'"

The counselor told me Bill's story as Bill had told it to him. (I will not share everything because of the graphic nature of the story.) He related how the drugs had taken over Bill's life and that on the night of the murder Bill and his companion were high and had been listening to heavy metal music. They decided to find someone, anyone, and watch him die. That night Bill murdered an innocent victim.

I realize that music was not the only contributing factor to the crime. I am simply relating a story as it was told to me that afternoon.

The counselor concluded by asking me to share this story while speaking on music and its influences whenever I felt it would help someone. He said Bill had asked him to relate it to as many as would listen so they wouldn't end up like him. I told the counselor I would share the story whenever I felt it was appropriate. I thanked him, walked to my car, and drove home with a heavy heart. I was sickened that a nineteen-year-old life had encountered and caused so much sorrow. I determined it was worth it to continue talking and writing positively about music and its many influences, regardless of the criticism, if it helped but one person.

Not long after my discussion with Bill's counselor, Bill was convicted of first-degree murder and sentenced to die for his crime. I will never forget watching the evening news as Bill gave his final plea for mercy before the sentence was read. His hair was cut neatly and he was dressed in a sharp-looking three-piece suit. The tears flowed as he read a written statement. He said he had learned many lessons since the crime and that for the first time in years he could see clearly without his mind being clouded by drugs and alcohol. He wanted his life to be of value to the youth of the country. He expressed his desire to help the youth understand the world of drugs, the occult, and heavy metal and punk rock music. He didn't want the lessons he'd learned to be wasted by killing him. As Bill finished his plea, the news clip then moved to the judge's response and the reading of the decision of the court. The judge simply stated, as accurately as I remember, "Your desires are admirable and I agree that you might be able to help other young people. However, your crime is so heinous that you will die for having committed it." What a tragedy! Nineteen years old and sentenced to death!

Sometime later, my teaching colleague wrote Bill and asked him how he got involved in everything. He asked about music, drugs, the occult, his turning point, his feelings about prison, and what he would do if he could change things. Bill responded quickly and asked the teacher to use his letter in any way he thought prudent. I would like to share just one item, which is pertinent to this book, in Bill's own words. It is his response to my colleague's question, How can the youth be careful about the music they listen to? What types of things should they avoid?

> This is a hard one! Let me first say this. Basically all music is evil. [I don't agree with Bill here. There is much of today's music that is good, positive, and uplifting.] What I mean is, even with the mellow bands that no one expects to be bad. The things they sing about such as money, cars, women, love. All those types of things help set a young person's morals and standards for life. So it's easy to say it's all bad. It works the same way.
>
> What should they avoid? It's pretty easy to see those things as long as their minds are clear. It's just the basic stuff. Album covers, bolts, chains, gravestones, violence, and basically the strange-looking covers. Groups that sing about death, violence, or the mystery of life. Basically just a gloomy outlook. Music with a lot of speed or a heavy sound played slow.

Bill's letter goes on and on. Question after question. But perhaps the real question is, will anyone listen to Bill's story and learn? Is there some way that Bill's tragic experience can be used to help someone from following the same path?

Again, the purpose of sharing Bill's story is not to suggest that everyone who listens to heavy metal, punk, or any other type of music with negative influences will become a murderer. But it does show what can happen if a person allows him- or herself to get beyond the feeling point. These are difficult times, and we must follow the Lord's servants in order to cling to the iron rod and partake of the fruit of the tree of life, whose fruit is "desirable to make one happy" (1 Nephi 8:10).

Elder Neal A. Maxwell taught this invaluable lesson: "Now we are entering times wherein there will be for all of us as Church members, in my judgment, some special challenges which will require of us that we follow the Brethren. All the easy things that the Church has had to do have been done. From now on, it's high adventure, and followership is going to be tested in some interesting ways."[7]

With all that is going on in the media and the music industry, wouldn't you say that we are involved in "high adventure"? With myriad choices to be made concerning our music, it can plainly be seen that our followership is being and will be tested. The real question is, will we have the courage to follow our leaders and the scriptural teachings, or will we fall by the wayside? In my judgment, the times in which we are now living are different and perhaps more challenging than any other in the earth's history. We must have the wisdom to follow.

Elder Boyd K. Packer made a request concerning music.

> I would recommend that you go through your record albums [may I also add CDs, tapes, and videos] and set aside those records that promote the so-called new morality, the drug, or the hard rock culture. Such music ought not to belong to young people concerned about spiritual development.
>
> Why not go through your collection? Get rid of the worst of it. Keep just the best of it. Be selective in what you consume and what you produce. It becomes a part of you.[8]

If we have to go through our collections and make some changes, then we must do it. We may not understand why at the present time, but we must learn to follow a prophet. Our prophets have spoken. President Ezra Taft Benson in October 1986 made the following statements concerning our entertainment and what the prophet Alma called the "lusts of your eyes" (see Alma 39:9):

"The lusts of your eyes." In our day, what does that expression mean? Movies, television programs, and video recordings that are both suggestive and lewd. Magazines and books that are obscene and pornographic.

We counsel you, young women [and men], not to pollute your minds with such degrading matter, for the mind through which this filth passes is never the same afterward. Don't see R-rated movies or vulgar videos or participate in any entertainment that is immoral, suggestive, or pornographic. And don't accept dates from young men who would take you to such entertainment. . . .

Instead, we encourage you to listen to uplifting music, both popular and classical, that builds the spirit. Learn some favorite hymns from our new hymnbook that build faith and spirituality. Attend dances where the music and the lighting and the dance movements are conducive to the Spirit. Watch those shows and entertainment that lift the spirit and promote clean thoughts and actions. Read books and magazines that do the same.[9]

President Benson made the Lord's position very clear. Obviously it's not an easy thing to follow and there are many who struggle with getting rid of that which appears to be so good and dear to the heart, yet inwardly is a spiritual onion. However, we must always remember that, as Elder Maxwell said, "someday, when we look back on mortality, we will see that so many of the things that seemed to matter so much at the moment will be seen not to have mattered at all. And the eternal things will be seen to have mattered even more than the most faithful of the Saints imagined."[10]

It is so easy at times to place a high priority on items that, in the eternal perspective, are not of much importance at all. We live in a world that oftentimes puts emphasis on material possessions rather than principles such as home, family, and spirituality. We cannot get so caught up in the world that we forget who we really are.

The Savior, while giving the Sermon on the Mount, told us who we are when he said, "Ye are the light of the world. A city that is set on an hill cannot be hid. Neither do men light a candle, and put it under a bushel, but on a candlestick; and it giveth light unto all that are in the house. Let your light so shine before men, that they may see your good works, and glorify your Father which is in heaven." (Matthew 5:14–16.)

President Spencer W. Kimball remarked: "You live in a time of wars and revolutions, yet the world will be revolutionized by the teaching of the gospel, which we must do . . . Women and men keeping the commandments of the Lord is the most revolutionary thing in the world."[11]

In relation to today's youth being a "light unto the world," President Benson again bore testimony, "It is my conviction that the Lord has held back some of his choicest spirits to come forth in this age so they could help prepare for that Second Coming."[12]

Can we not see that truth has been given to many so they can light the way for an ailing world? Wouldn't it be a tragedy if those who had the truth let their lights go out and the world lost its way, more so than it already has, because their music or other forms of entertainment dimmed their spirits?

When it comes to making changes in our music and other forms of entertainment, my mind turns to the story of Naaman and Elisha as told in 2 Kings 5. Naaman, a captain of the host of the king of Syria, was a great, honorable, and courageous man. He was loved dearly by the king of Syria but suffered one major problem: he was a leper.

Fortunately for him, his wife had a "little maid" who knew of the prophet in Israel and communicated this message to the correct people in hopes of having this mighty man healed.

When the king heard the story, he, because of his great love for Naaman, insisted that Naaman go to Israel and be healed. He sent a letter to the king of Israel explaining the problem and his desire to have his friend healed of leprosy.

When Naaman approached the king of Israel, the king was disturbed because of his inadequacies, saying, "Am I God, to kill and to make alive, that this man doth send unto me to recover a man of his leprosy?" (Verse 7.) The king couldn't heal him and he knew it.

However, Elisha the prophet heard about this confrontation and sent for Naaman. When Naaman arrived in all of his honor and glory, he stood at the door of the house of Elisha, undoubtedly expecting a magnificent reception and honoring. To the contrary, the prophet sent a messenger with a very simple request to have Naaman "go and wash in Jordan seven times, and thy flesh shall come again to thee, and thou shalt be clean" (verse 10).

Naaman was furious at such a seemingly stupid request. He stormed away angry and upset, declaring that the rivers in Damascus were far superior to any in Israel. He was offended by the request of a prophet.

Then something very interesting happened. "And his servants came near, and spake unto him, and said, My father, if the prophet had bid thee do some great thing, wouldest thou not have done it? how much rather then, when he saith to thee, Wash, and be clean? Then went he down, and dipped himself seven times in Jordan, according to the saying of the man of God: and his flesh came again like unto the flesh of a little child, and he was clean." (2 Kings 5:13–14.)

He then returned to Elisha, giving thanks and praising the God of Israel. How much like Naaman are we when a man of God, a prophet, asks us to do something so simple as to go through our records, CDs, tapes, and videos and set aside that which is inappropriate and hinders spiritual development? Do we feel that we know better than a prophet? Do we lack the faith to understand that obedience, or the lack of it, does affect our spiritual development?

I'm sure that if the prophet "bid thee do some great thing," such as serve as a mission president, stake president, athletic star, movie star, bishop, General Authority, or millionaire, "wouldest thou not have done it?"

If we are so willing to do the "great things," what about doing the simple things, such as paying tithing, serving missions, working on the welfare farm, praying, or even getting rid of inappropriate music or videos?

Remember, when Naaman repented and followed the man of God, his leprosy was healed and he was blessed. The Lord wants to heal and bless our lives if we but learn to follow and be obedient. He has told us, "I, the Lord, am bound when ye do what I say; but when ye do not what I say, ye have no promise" (D&C 82:10).

Hopefully, in this matter of music and other forms of entertainment, it will not be said of you or me as it was the young rich man who approached Jesus with a question of what he had to do to gain eternal life. Jesus replied, "Keep the commandments." The young man inquired which commandments he should keep, and Jesus told him. "The young man saith unto him, All these have I kept from my youth up: what lack I yet? Jesus said unto him, . . . go and sell that thou hast, . . . and come and follow me. But when the young man heard that saying, he went away sorrowful: for he had great possessions." (Matthew 19:16–22.)

Wouldn't it be tragic if anyone were to say, "I'm sorry, Lord, I can't follow what thou hast asked of me concerning music, because I just have too much money invested in inappropriate CDs, tapes, records, and videos. It would simply cost too much to weed out my collection."

Hopefully all people everywhere will have the wisdom and the courage to "come listen to a prophet's voice."

And ye shall know the truth,
and the truth shall make you free.
—John 8:32

8

Never Fearing Truth

As this book comes to a close we must refer to a concept mentioned in the opening chapter—that of never fearing truth. I mention this concept again because it is so vital in making correct and courageous decisions. God needs brave sons and daughters. Being brave and standing for truth and righteousness is never easy. It takes courage to always live truth and resist temptation. But it can be done. The Apostle Paul taught, "There hath no temptation taken you but such as is common to man: but God is faithful, who will not suffer you to be tempted above that you are able; but will with the temptation also make a way to escape, that ye may be able to bear it" (1 Corinthians 10:13). If God provides a way to avoid temptation, how do we overcome it and conquer it? The Savior taught that we must "watch and pray always lest ye enter into temptation; for Satan desireth to have you, that he may sift you as wheat" (3 Nephi 18:18). Praying to avoid temptation, however, is only one way to conquer it. Another is to simply never go near it or flirt with it. Elder Joseph B. Wirthlin of the Quorum of the Twelve Apostles taught us well on this topic:

> Willing obedience provides lasting protection against Satan's alluring and tantalizing temptations. Jesus is our per-

fect example of obedience. Learn to do as He did when Satan tempted Him in the wilderness. Even though He was weakened by fasting, His answer was quick and firm: "Get thee behind me, Satan" (Luke 4:8). Elder Neal A. Maxwell said this of the Savior's example in resisting temptation: "Jesus noticed the tremendous temptations that came to Him, but He did not process and reprocess them. Instead, He rejected them promptly. If we entertain temptations, soon they begin entertaining us!" (*Ensign,* May 1987, p. 71.) When Satan comes calling, cast him out as quickly as possible. Do not let temptation even begin to entertain you.[1]

To illustrate this point and tie the entire book together I would like to tell a story that I have told many times but that bears repeating again. It occurred many years ago while I was speaking in Washington State at a youth conference held at a mountain resort. As a result of pondering on this story often, I have on occasion gained strength to make correct decisions. Perhaps the retelling of the story may help you as you make the music decision and stand tall in the face of truth about music and other forms of entertainment.

The air had a smell of pine and a mixture of wildflowers. The pleasant rolling sound of a nearby stream greeted my ears as I walked along the gray and white gravel path, enjoying the various aromas and sounds of the forest. I felt the familiar excitement of speaking at a youth conference come in the form of sweaty palms and butterflies in the pit of my stomach. For some unknown reason I was particularly nervous as I walked along the dimly lit path. During the preceding years I had spoken many, many times on music and its effects on our actions, feelings, thoughts, and spirituality. So why be nervous now? The fireside was scheduled late in the evening and the young people were very tired, and a lecture on a topic as sensitive as music would be difficult. The fact that so many would be coming with preconceived biases and walls of defense set up had apparently put me a little on edge. The influence of the Spirit was desperately needed, for "if ye receive not the Spirit ye shall not teach" (D&C 42:14). By having the Spirit, these walls could be broken down.

I tried to concentrate on the sweet smells and sounds of the forest as I walked, in hopes of relaxing somewhat. I glanced at my watch but couldn't see the time because the tall pine trees hanging over the path blocked most of the moonlight. I held my right arm in the air in hopes that one of the dim path lights would aid me. It did. The time to begin the fireside was not far away, so I picked up my pace and hurried toward the main conference gathering place.

As I approached the arena, stereo cassette player and briefcase in hand, I noticed four young men standing under a path light, listening intensely to some music. It wasn't difficult to tell what type of music they were playing as the heavy metal sounds screamed out through the night air. Chuckling to myself, I thought, *Man, these guys are really getting spiritually prepared to hear my message.* Putting my briefcase and stereo under one arm, I headed towards them, hoping to shake hands and give them a little bit of a hard time, all in fun.

As I approached, the boy holding the industrial-sized stereo on his shoulder set it down and started walking towards me. How do I describe him? He was not very tall, maybe 5′5″ or 5′6″ at the most. His hair was—well, unique. Three or four styles all on one head. From his left ear dangled an earring. He wore a black leather jacket with a small chain over one shoulder. Both wrists were circled with spiked wristbands. His black T-shirt bore the logo of a heavy metal band that I assumed he had bought at one of their concerts.

As the distance between us narrowed I smiled, said hello, and stretched out my hand to shake his. Instead of shaking hands he completely surprised me by slapping my hand to the side and poking me in the center of the chest with his right forefinger. As his finger was pressing against my tie, he began to shake his rear end back and forth while asking me a startling question. "Are you the chump that's going to tell us all our rock 'n' roll music is bad and if we listen to heavy metal we're all going to hell?"

What could I say? It wasn't clear to me if he was serious or if he had just beat me to the punch and was giving me a hard time, in jest, before I could do it to him. The whole situation took me by surprise.

I told him, "Yeah, I'm the speaker, and I'm speaking on music, but I'm not going to tell you what I think is good and bad in music. I'd like to show you how to choose appropriately and how music affects your actions, feelings, thoughts, and spirituality and then let you make your own decisions about what you will or will not listen to."

Without waiting for more he took aim again with his finger and poked me in the chest a second time. Again with his finger on my tie, he asked basically the same question: "Listen, Mr. Chump, are you going to tell us all our heavy metal is bad and if we listen to rock 'n' roll we're all going to hell?"

By this time I was trying to suppress my irritation, because I was beginning to realize he wasn't just kidding around. I started to shake and could feel the tips of my ears getting hot.

I responded, "I'm only going to tell you two things, partner. Number one, please don't touch me again, and number two, please don't call me chump, because you are really starting to irritate me."

I had no sooner said those words, when *bam!* his finger made contact with my chest a third time. With a somewhat raised voice he said, "If you tell me heavy metal music or my rock 'n' roll is bad, I'll get up and I'll leave your discussion!"

In my mind I reasoned, *If that's all it takes, he is as good as gone!*

He walked away saying somewhat jokingly, "I'll leave! I'll leave!" I couldn't resist, so I yelled back, motioning towards him with the back of my hand, "Go ahead and leave, son. Go ahead and leave!"

When I finally reached the location where the fireside was to be held, I prayed desperately for the Spirit to be with me and tried to gather my thoughts after my unsettling encounter in the forest. When I stood up to speak and looked at the audience, there sat my young "friend" with all his little buddies. They were on the second row directly in front of where I had to stand and speak for the next hour and a half. I tried to ignore them, but it was a little difficult to do with each of them sitting with folded arms and eyes glaring the message, *Go ahead, chump, just try and tell us anything is wrong with our music. Try and teach us or make us change!*

I had been speaking for about forty-five minutes when the time for me to talk about learning how to choose arrived. I quoted some verses from the seventh chapter of Moroni. While doing so, the before-mentioned phrase from the film *Man's Search for Happiness* raced through my mind: "Only if you are unafraid of truth will you ever find it." I had heard that phrase many times in the past and had even used it in several of my talks. But never before had it come into my mind with such force. That seemed to be the answer. How would anyone ever find truth if they feared it?

With this thought, I quoted the phrase with emphasis and then did something I had never done before nor since. I looked directly at the young man and repeated the phrase. "Only if you are unafraid of truth will you ever find it." I wanted to call him a chump but didn't. Not taking my eyes off of him, I said, "Young man, you are afraid of the truth, and until you have the courage to face it and not fear it, it will elude you forever!"

He glared back as if to say, *How dare you say that to me.*

I glared right back, saying to myself, *How dare I say that?* We both were shocked.

After the bold stares, he bowed his head in silence and did not look up at me again for the remainder of the talk. Now the audience was captivated! You could have heard a pin drop. My head felt hot as I felt the pressure of their eyes.

The first of a series of questions I presented pierced the tense silence. "Young people, are you afraid of truth? Does it embarrass you, or are you ashamed to be a member of the true church of Jesus Christ? Are you uncomfortable with the fact that you are supposed to live life differently from the rest of the world? Does it bother you to be identified with cleanli-

ness, goodness, and virtue? Do you struggle with the standard
that says you are not to be involved in immorality, drugs, or alcohol like so many in the world? Truth will require sacrifice
and may be difficult on the ego. Do you have the courage it
takes to live truth?"

Most in attendance, including me, were stunned with the
straightforwardness of my questioning. These deep, penetrating questions led us into an exciting discussion about the val-
ues and difficulties associated with finding and living truth.

We quoted the words of the Apostle Peter from 2 Peter
2:1–2 concerning false teachers teaching that "the way of truth
shall be evil spoken of." We determined that living the truth
would not be easy. We talked of the change that may come
about as a result of truth and how change requires stretching.
Leaving the comfort zone is very difficult. But the Savior taught
that by knowing and living the truth, we would actually find
freedom (see John 8:32). This freedom paves the way for us to
have the Spirit and rid ourselves of the shackles of deception.
"For the Spirit speaketh the truth and lieth not. Wherefore, it
speaketh of things as they really are, and of things as they really
will be." (Jacob 4:13.)

As our discussion on truth ended and we headed back to
the assigned topic of music and how it affects us, I noticed that
the young man on the second row still had his head down and
would not look at me. Inside I hoped I had not offended him
but was certain I had. I felt like Nephi talking to Laman and
Lemuel. They complained that he had spoken hard things to
them, but he responded that he "knew that I had spoken hard
things against the wicked, according to the truth; . . . wherefore, the guilty taketh the truth to be hard, for it cutteth them
to the very center" (1 Nephi 16:2). I wasn't sure he had been
cut to the "very center," but I knew something was going on
inside him. The talk ended on a very positive note, yet he still
refused to look at me.

After the meeting was over I stood in front of the pulpit
talking and shaking hands with some of the youth and their
leaders. It wasn't long before I noticed the young man from

the second row standing in line, waiting, I thought, to shake my hand and talk. When he reached the front of the line, he raised his finger, the same one he had poked me in the chest with, and started waving it in my face. But this time he didn't touch me. "I want to talk with you, mister! Alone!"

Great, I thought. *He probably wants to kill me after embarrassing him in front of all his friends.*

We arranged for a time the following morning just before breakfast. I knew it would be light and there would be lots of people around. He left. I went on shaking hands.

It wasn't too long before I left the building and headed for my sleeping quarters about half a mile away through the trees. It was very pleasant to walk through the pines again and smell the familiar smells that had greeted me a few hours earlier. The path was once again lit by the dim path lights, and a faint moon was trying to make its way through a few scattered late night clouds.

I hadn't gone far when I noticed someone standing behind a tree, watching me. My heart began to pound and my palms to sweat when I recognized the haircut. It was my young "friend."

Maybe he really is going to kill me, I thought as he walked slowly in my direction.

Before either of us spoke, my mind began to do crazy things. I started thinking of all the things I would do if he tried anything tricky. My heart felt as though it was in my throat. It was pounding with anticipation as he approached.

"Brother Christianson, could I have a few minutes of your time before you go to bed?" His voice was soft now and subdued. His eyes did not look anywhere but at his shoes. "I'm afraid if I wait until morning I won't have the courage to talk to you."

"Sure," I said, knowing he could probably detect my nervousness by the shakiness of my voice. "Before we talk, could I have two things from you first?"

"Yeah, I guess so."

"First of all, what's your name?"

"Jim," he said, almost muffling his voice. "Could we find a place to sit down? This might take awhile." Little did I know then, as we walked back down the lighted path towards the kitchen area, just how long it would be. We spotted a large piece of concrete in a small bunch of trees just off the path. It was right below a light, so I felt pretty safe. Our talk lasted almost three complete hours.

"Well, Jim, the second thing I'd like to ask is for your forgiveness. Will you please forgive me for embarrassing you in front of all your friends?"

"Maybe I needed it," he answered rudely, his eyes now glaring at me, no longer looking at his shoes.

Well, excuse me! I thought as I glared right back. I sat on the concrete, somewhat uncomfortable with his Dr. Jekyll and Mr. Hyde behavior.

The silence was killing me as we sat there, but I didn't know what to say about what had just happened. Finally, mustering some courage, I asked, "What do you mean you needed it?" He didn't hesitate with his reply.

"Tonight, for the first time in my life, I asked myself if I was afraid of truth."

"What did you find out?" I asked, somewhat sarcastically.

"I'm terrified!" he cried. His head sagged again towards the ground. He tried to stop the tears with the back of his hand, but it was too late. They were already on their way off the end of his nose and chin and had dripped onto the concrete block.

"If I live the truth, Brother Christianson, I have to give up every one of my friends, in the Church and out."

"You don't have to give up all of them, do you?" I asked innocently.

"I said all of them!" Again, I was stunned by his sudden change in behavior. Here he was yelling at me through his tears, and all I wanted to do was help the poor guy.

"Every one of my friends is involved in drugs or alcohol or both." He glanced at me briefly with a pained look in his eyes and then hid his face behind his arm, which was wrapped around his knee.

"Are you involved, Jim?" Again the tears started to flow as he explained to me about his involvement. I cried and my heart ached as I listened to his sad story.

After we discussed his problems concerning drugs and alcohol, we launched into another deep discussion. Jim said, "After listening to you speak tonight, if I live the truth I think I have to get rid of all my music."

"Now wait a minute, Slick," I said jokingly. "I never told you to get rid of *all* your music."

Apparently that's all it took to set him off again. He yelled, "I said I have to get rid of all of it!"

Go ahead, burn the whole pile, you ornery little beggar! I thought to myself as I contemplated how to ask him the next question without upsetting him. "Why do you have to get rid of all of it?"

He didn't even flinch with his answer. "Because my music makes me feel exactly the way I want to feel."

"How's that?"

"Angry!"

"Why?"

"Because I hate my dad!" With this admission, his lower lip started to quiver and the tears began once more.

We both sat in silence under the light while he regained his composure. The various sounds and smells of the crisp mountain air seemed to bring courage and comfort as we began a lengthy discussion concerning the many difficulties of his home life. As we discussed the situation in his home, too personal to write about, he surprised me once more with a penetrating question. His voice was shaky, and with a deliberate hesitancy he asked, "Would you be my dad?"

"Uh . . . yeah . . . I guess so. What do you mean by that?" I spoke before my mind had an opportunity to contemplate all that being the "father" of a troubled fourteen-year-old boy would entail.

"I don't want to come and live with you or anything like that," he said, bringing much relief to my heart. "I just want you to call me on the phone or come and see me when you come this way again. I guess I just want you to help me live the truth. Can you do that?" he pleaded while his eyes looked at me like one of my own children asking for a special favor.

"Sure, Jim. I'd be honored to help any way I can."

By the time we had discussed Jim's family problems the night had moved into the early morning hours. I was extremely tired and definitely ready for bed, but Jim still needed to talk.

"Before you go to bed, Brother Christianson, I have one more thing to tell you. If I live the truth, I think I have to go and talk to my bishop. Are you a bishop?" There was hope in his voice.

"Yes, but I'm not your bishop," I answered quickly.

He was quick to interject, "You see, my bishop knows my mom, and I know if I go to him she'll find out everything. How about if I tell you everything, and it'll be our little secret?"

"I wish it were that easy. You can tell me if you want, but you still have to talk to your own bishop."

He looked off into the trees and then slowly turned his head towards me. It was obvious an idea was churning in his mind.

"How about if I tell you everything I've done and then you tell me if I need to go or not, and if I don't I won't? Sound like a deal?"

"That's fine, but you'll have to hurry because I can hardly keep my eyes open." I realized I was in for quite a story.

Again we discussed items too personal to write about. He didn't leave out anything as far as I could tell. I sat on the rock in wonderment, trying to imagine how a fourteen-year-old boy could have been involved so deeply in so many things of the world. When he finished, he very confidently asked, "Well, what do you think? Do you think I ought to go talk with my bishop or not?"

I cleared my throat and weakly said, "Hurry!" He said he would soon but would commit to nothing definite.

By this time I couldn't stay awake. I stood up from the rock, swatted him affectionately on the shoulder, and let him know we'd have to finish in the morning.

I started to walk away and had only walked fifteen or twenty paces when I received the greatest shock of the evening. "Brother Christianson," he called out, "would you think it was crazy if I gave you a hug?"

I turned and saw his unusual haircut silhouetted in the light behind the rock. The shadows hid his face, but I could tell he was serious.

"Get over here," I lovingly said as I motioned for him to come to me.

What followed next I have never been able to forget or erase from my memory. He put his arms around me, rested his head on my chest, and hugged me tightly, as if he were my own child. We both sobbed as we stood there on the path.

He only wanted to know three simple things: Could he be forgiven? Was it all really worth it? Would I promise to help him live the truth? As I fought back tears and the large lump in my throat, all I could muster was one feeble "yes" to each question. We walked arm in arm for a few steps down the path and made some very special promises to one another concerning truth. We both realized then how difficult it would be to find and live the truth when so many were mocking and fearing it.

The now familiar sounds and smells of that forest almost seemed to communicate their agreement. Truth would require change and would be a very difficult and lifelong process. Jim had a long way to go in his quest but had overcome one of the major hurdles. He was learning not to fear it. He was willing, for the time being, to pay whatever price was necessary.

The following morning after breakfast I prepared to leave the mountain resort and head back to Salt Lake City. As I climbed into the car and sat down on the sun-heated seat, I heard the sound of music and laughter filter through the trees. The thought hit me that no one at the conference but Jim and me was aware of what had taken place on a concrete block adjacent to the pathway in a small bunch of trees.

As I asked myself about the reality of Jim's keeping his commitment to live the truth, I saw him running towards the car. I closed the door and rolled down the window.

"You promised me you'd help me live the truth and that you'd call and write me," he said as he stood beside the car with his thumbs hooked inside the front pockets of his jeans.

"Yes, I did, my friend, and I will." Before rolling up the window I stretched out my arm and shook his hand. "I'll look forward to hearing from you real soon, buddy." He acknowledged the statement with a nod of his head and stood watching as I drove out of sight.

The air-conditioning felt cool and refreshing as it blew against my bare face and arms. As I rode along the winding road that made its way out of the mountains toward the airport, I thought of Jim and what we had just experienced. For some reason I also thought of Lehi and his vision of the great and spacious building. "And great was the multitude that did enter into that strange building. And after they did enter into that building they did point the finger of scorn at me and those that were partaking of the fruit also; but we heeded them not." (1 Nephi 8:33.) I came to the realization that many would mock and seek to destroy Jim's attempt to live the truth, not only concerning music, but also in every other area of his life.

I have not seen Jim since that afternoon. We have communicated by mail, and he has given me permission to share this story. His courage to face the truth and try to live it has given me great courage and a desire to follow his example.

The purpose of this book has not been to tear down any particular type of music. It has been to educate and hopefully edify the reader. Much has been written in recent years about the many challenges associated with contemporary music, its artists, and the lifestyles it promotes. News articles, firesides, and lectures on the subject have become commonplace. It is quite simple to find something wrong with almost anything if you look hard or long enough. That has not been my objective. My objective has been to teach the truth as I understand it and to encourage the reader to choose for him- or herself. However, when choosing for ourselves and exercising agency, we must remember that accepting responsibility for those choices, good or bad, becomes vital. Each individual must accept and live with the consequences of his or her decisions and choices. One cannot escape it.

Just before Jesus was put to death Pilate asked him, "What is truth?" This question followed Jesus' statement, "To this end was I born, and for this cause came I into the world, that I should bear witness unto the truth. Every one that is of the truth heareth my voice." (John 18:37–38.)

If Jesus answered on this occasion, it was not recorded. Centuries later, however, he gave a thought-provoking answer to the Prophet Joseph Smith: "And truth is knowledge of things as they are, and as they were, and as they are to come" (D&C 93:24). Truth about music, videos, other entertainment, or anything else in life is the same yesterday, today, and forever. It can be found. It is available to all who do not fear it.

Music is love in search of a word.
—Sidney Lanier

For Parents and Youth Leaders: A Solution

A few years ago I met a young man who helped me gain a greater appreciation for the power of good music. I was in the process of completing graduate school when one of my fellow students asked me a question concerning my speaking and writing about music.

As we discussed some of the research I had done he mentioned that he knew a boy from Colorado whose emotional life had been saved by music. Ironically, the boy and his parents were staying at one of the local dorms while his father attended summer school. He asked if I would like to meet the boy. Of course, I was very interested. A time was arranged for us to meet at the dorm later that afternoon.

As we walked through the door of the dorm I was greeted by a boy just under six years of age who was terribly scarred on his head, arms, and hands. He stretched forth his hand to shake mine and said, "Hello, mister. My name is Luke Jones. What's yours?" I told him my name, and the man who had brought me told Luke why I had come. He said, "That's great. I gotta go play with my friends. See ya later. Have a wonderful day."

I was surprised and shocked. His outgoing manner was refreshing. His parents were just as sweet and kind. After a brief introduction they showed me a video of Luke's life and accomplishments. They told me he was part of the Children's Miracle Network Telethon and shared the story of how he came to be in his current condition. They informed me that music was one of the greatest influences in Luke's young life. When Luke became frustrated or overly excited he would sing. The singing would calm him down and his frustrations would flee. He also struggled at times with recalling material he had learned, but when listening to or playing music on the piano, his recall significantly increased.

It was amazing that music could play such a vital role in the life of someone so young. But as the story unfolded it became much more clear how powerful and wonderful good, wholesome music can be in each of our lives and why it is so vital that we have it.

When Luke was eighteen months old he had a tragic accident while sitting on the edge of his mother's washing machine. A load of wash had just been placed in the washer, when Luke's mother was called to take care of other sick children. In her haste, she momentarily forgot about Luke sitting on the washing machine. Immediately upon realizing she had left Luke in a dangerous position, she ran back to the washroom. To her horror, she saw that Luke had fallen headfirst into the swirling machine. She removed him and administered first aid, trying to revive him and save his life. After the ambulance finally arrived, Luke was rushed to the local hospital.

He spent four months in intensive care, having suffered three major injuries. Sixty percent of his little body had been burned by the scalding water. He had all but drowned, as well as suffering severe head injuries from being beaten with the paddles of the washer. Very few people thought Luke would live. But he did. After leaving the hospital he wore a rubber mask and hat for eighteen months to cover his severe scarring.

Finally, when his mother felt it was time for Luke to interact with other children, she was extremely concerned. Both she and her husband had great fear that Luke would have a difficult time adjusting to being with other children, and that they would have a difficult time adjusting to him and his new appearance as well.

At this time Luke's mother was serving as Primary president. She decided to discuss Luke's situation with his Sunbeam teacher. With great confidence in the teacher, this faithful mother asked if the teacher would take special care of Luke and help him adjust to this very trying situation.

When Luke entered the Primary class for the first time, his appearance particularly frightened one little girl. She screamed with fear and started going into hysterics. She would not stop. In desperation the teacher, trying to calm the girl down and also trying to assure the other class members that everything was under control, had Luke come to the front of the class and pull up his rubber mask. She calmly said, "Now, see, boys and girls, Luke is a real boy. He's just like you." The other children were so intrigued by what they saw under the mask that they rushed towards Luke to get a closer look. This sudden rush of movement and attention frightened him. The children pressed upon him, trying to see what was under his covering, while the little girl continued her screaming in a distant corner.

Luke began to panic. The only way he knew to calm his fear and frustration was to do what he had always done: to sing. With a quivering voice, in this moment of need and fear, this sweet little boy began to sing "I Am a Child of God." The teacher told his mother that the class joined in and finished singing this beautiful prayer unto God. The music so soothed the class that by the end of the meeting, Luke was coloring in a book with the little girl who had been so hysterical. The song from a little boy's heart, his plea to God for help, his remembering who he was and calling upon God in his own way, through music, caused a calmness and peace to come upon the entire room and each individual. It also was an answer to his parents' prayers that Luke could be successful as his life progressed. This heavenly experience brought peace and joy to all who were involved in it. Each of us could learn a valuable lesson from little Luke Jones.

Music, when used appropriately, can bring peace, comfort, and joy. This true principle not only worked for Luke Jones but it can work for you and me as we go through the rigors of daily living. Are we using the beautiful powers of music to aid us in getting answers to our prayers, and has music been the answer to many a parent's prayer as it was for the Joneses? Was it the music that allowed Luke to truly believe, in a time of trial, that he was a son of God? Was this music teaching the same sermon the Savior so eloquently taught when he said, "Remember the worth of souls is great in the sight of God" (D&C 18:10)? Even a six-year-old boy's prayer in song was heard by the God of the universe.

Every single soul is precious to God. We must never forget this while dealing with music, especially while dealing with those whose music is contributing to their inability to receive answers in their times of need. We cannot rest until each of our Father's sheep is brought safely into the arms of the true Shepherd. Just one young man or woman does make a difference, and I, for one, can hardly bear to see one of them, regardless of his or her problems, standing on the outside wondering how to weather the storms of life. We cannot afford to lose one of our youth or their parents to the powers of inappropriate music.

Horace Mann made the statement at the dedication of a boys' home that if all the work and energy and money put into the endeavor saved but one boy, it would be worth it. He was then questioned by someone as being insincere and becoming too oratorical. "Oh, yes, I meant it," Horace Mann insisted. "It would have all been worth it, if the one were my son."[1] Again, we cannot stop until all people are brought within the influence of the Master.

Without question, many people have already progressed beyond the feeling point, having rejected much of what the gospel offers. Yet we must not cease trying to bring them back.

Too often we forget that the most important factor in dealing with music, or any other difficult issue, is people. It is the individual who is of ultimate worth.

People often comment to me that if they applied the thirteenth article of faith correctly, and Moroni 7, and Elder Packer's teachings, they would never be able to listen to any music in the "popular" category. I disagree. I often tune my radio to what I judge to be acceptable popular music. I simply reserve the right to change stations if an inappropriate song is played.

As in all decisions of discernment, the Spirit must become our guide. This means that we must use wisdom and love in guiding those who struggle with difficult choices in music. Alma's words to his son Shiblon are appropriate: "Use boldness, but not overbearance; and also see that ye bridle all your passions, that ye may be filled with love" (Alma 38:12).

We must be bold, but never overbearing. In our counseling we must be filled with love, and we must allow people to do things of their own free will and choice. They may choose contrary to what we think is best for them. However, we must be bold. We cannot be afraid of our children or fear that they might get angry and run away. Child development experts suggest that parents must take charge. They must take the lead and show the way for their children.[2]

President Dwight D. Eisenhower understood this principle. To illustrate it, in a Cabinet meeting he would lay a long piece of string on the table. He would pick up one end of the string and try to push it forward. It would always become entangled. Then he would pull the string and it would follow freely.

Somehow, if we can gently lead, if we can pull rather than push people along—teaching by example, love, and patience—perhaps many will follow.

What will happen in our homes when posters of inappropriate artists go up on bedroom walls, when styles shift to dramatic clothing and hairstyles, when school grades drop and the sweet nature of our child turns irritable? How will we handle such a situation? Here is where I believe we need to take charge, but we must do it in an appropriate way. Hopefully no parent or guardian would be unwise enough to go into a young person's room and destroy record albums and tapes or tear down everything on the wall without consulting with the child first. We must reason together. We must begin to ask questions as to why certain drastic changes in behavior are taking place.

Robert Coles, a Harvard child psychiatrist, has said, "If strong family or church life is absent, what other moral influences are there?" Other experts suggest that some of the vast behavioral changes are signals that adults should notice when entertainment threatens emotional health.[3]

Darlyne Pettinicchio, cofounder of Back in Control Training Center in Fullerton, California, has suggested that music is the number one indicator of emotional problems. "The troubled kids will be totally absorbed in either heavy-metal or punk music," she said. Then she suggested that a rebellious stage sets in. Some even become physically violent and very aggressive, responding to their parents with the "you can't tell me what to do" attitude. Hairstyles change drastically and their clothing becomes very dark. Pettinicchio and other experts suggest that enforcing rules for school attendance and household chores is vital, and, if necessary, there may even be a ban on certain types of music. She does suggest that, yes, the teenager may get upset, but you have to give clear, direct commands and signals. However, we must be extremely wise and intelligent in how we go about this process.[4]

Dr. Bruno Bettelheim, who taught at the University of Chicago for many years and was an internationally known child psychologist, has suggested that if a child is addicted to a certain kind of music or to a certain musical group, it means there is a gap in the child's life that he or she is trying to fill.

"Many teenagers turn up their hi-fis full blast to blast other thoughts out of their heads," he said. "It is a way of getting away from troubling feelings or to fill a void. It's similar to an addiction to drugs. People become addicted not because drugs are around but because of emptiness. If everything in a young person's life is in order, then the media will have very little influence."

Dr. Bettelheim goes on to say, "A teenager has to make judgments based on quality. But he cannot do that by himself. He needs help, and to provide it parents must have good judgment themselves. If they watch [or listen to] trash, how are they going to develop a child's judgment?"[5] Usually whatever is the most popular entertainment of the time is blamed for everything, but much in the media can be made constructive if parents take an interest.

As Latter-day Saints we must be holding regular, quality family home evenings on the subject. Issues of music could be regularly mentioned in family prayers and scripture study. If we have patient faith, the Lord will aid us. If we teach our children diligently, I believe he will keep his promises and cause that his "grace shall attend you" (D&C 88:78). He will bless us but not when we overreact in a fit of anger or impatience. President Ezra Taft Benson said:

> Games should be played which develop the mental, physical, and/or spiritual qualities of family members. Singing songs and hymns can be a means of bringing inspiring music into the home and of helping each child to build his own musical vocabulary. Many parents have simply turned the musical education of their children over to the local rock radio station, with increasingly unpleasant results. Most children are delighted to discover music of genuine merit when their parents help to make it available to them. Bringing great music into the home can be an enriching and exciting experience not only for children but for parents as well.[6]

The best advice I have ever heard on handling the subject comes from the analogy of a young child picking up a sharp object. Sometimes a foolish adult will grab for it, frightened for the safety of the child. Instinctively the child may grip it more tightly and perhaps injure him- or herself or the parent as he or she pulls away. The wise parent will offer some equally appealing but harmless object in exchange so that the child will let go willingly and without tears.

We must keep that in mind when we have a problem with young people and their music. To change it may take some time and require a great deal of inspiration.

Helping people to change requires persuasion, long-suffering, gentleness, meekness, love unfeigned, and kindness (see D&C 121:41–42). We must provide constructive and interesting alternatives. We must keep in mind "to tell is to preach, to ask is to teach."

The question arises, then: if our young people and adults change their music habits, with what do they replace their former tastes? Perhaps the question can be answered with another question: Why aren't more Latter-day Saints composing and producing music that is appropriate? President Heber J. Grant in a way implied that same question: "I wish that as far as possible we would get into the habit of singing our own music, that is, music composed by our own people."[7]

One of the major solutions to the musical dilemma, in my opinion, is to flood the market with wholesome, edifying music. Why should we sit back idly and allow the adversary nearly total control of this most powerful medium? As a people we must contribute more to what today's youth, as well as adults, listen to by writing, composing, and producing music that meets the Lord's approval.

Elder Orson F. Whitney thought this possible. "We shall yet have Miltons and Shakespeares of our own. God's ammunition is not exhausted. His highest spirits are held in reserve for the latter times. In God's name and by His help we will build up a literature whose tops will touch the heaven, though its foundation may now be low on the earth."[8]

I believe we shall have not only Miltons and Shakespeares but Beethovens and Bachs as well. We must believe in ourselves and have hope in our abilities. We must seek to live clean lives in order to receive the inspiration necessary to compose music that will be not only appealing to our people but edifying as well. We must always remember that "the brightest lights shine from the cleanest instruments."

Some Latter-day Saints have taken the challenge and are producing and performing wonderful, inspiring music. To those I say, thank you for enriching my life and satisfying the needs of the young people. Thank you for making the music decision easier and more rewarding. However, we need many more Latter-day Saints to make this much needed contribution in the vital area of popular music.

Perhaps one reason our people do not produce more good music is that we as a people do not seek eagerly enough the Spirit to guide our pens but rather seek to please the world. Elder Packer has instructed us well in this matter:

> It is a mistake to assume that one can follow the ways of the world and then somehow, in a moment of intruded inspiration, compose a great anthem of the Restoration, or in a moment of singular inspiration paint the great painting. When it is done, it will be done by one who has yearned and tried and longed fervently to do it, not by one who has condescended to do it. It will take quite as much preparation and work as any masterpiece, and a different kind of inspiration.[9]

As was stated earlier, perhaps the greatest songs, hymns, and anthems have not yet been composed. Elder Packer stated, "When they are produced, who will produce them? . . . They will be produced by those who are the most inspired among us."[10] Note that this line does not say "the most famous" or "the most talented," but "the most inspired"—those who not only have sought to communicate the will of the Lord but have lived according to his mind and will.

Too often, perhaps, we do not achieve all we could in using our musical talents because we worry about pleasing the world rather than God (see Galatians 5:26). There is as much responsibility on the performer as there is on the listener (see D&C 50:17–22). If we could bear equal responsibility, we would accomplish much in the way of a solution to our "music problem."

President Joseph Fielding Smith remarked on the principle of singleness of purpose. "Now if you understand the gospel of Jesus Christ, it will make you free. If your softball, your volleyball, your basketball, your foot racing, your dancing, your other entertainments are devoid of the Spirit of the Lord, they will be of no value to you. . . . Do everything with an eye single unto the glory of God, and let us teach to build up and strengthen ourselves and The Church of Jesus Christ of Latter-day Saints."[11]

If we could do this, I am confident that our music and other arts would become a standard to the good people of the world.

In summary, these are some of the basic keys to a solution:

1. Take charge of the situation; teach, exhort, expound.
2. Provide creative, interesting alternatives.
3. Be wise in how we go about helping our young people with their music.
4. Follow the teachings of the scriptures and of the living prophets in the standards they set for choosing.
5. Flood the market with that which is good.
6. Seek the Spirit of the Lord in all we do.

It is also suggested that all people who desire to influence people for good and who wish to nurture and perfect their musical abilities have the courage to do just that! Such individuals should not become bogged down in the unworthy music of our day. They should have faith in God and in themselves. Each of us is a son or daughter of God, and we have within us the abilities to become instruments in God's hands to achieve that which is good.

I have faith that this can be done. We can be a light for all the world to follow in the ever growing darkness if each of us will choose to follow the Lord in our choices in music, as well as in all our pursuits in life.

I love the statement, "Following the prophet is not always easy, but it is always right." I have come to know that truer words were never spoken. "For only if we are unafraid of truth will we ever find it."[12]

My friends, the decision is yours. Each person must decide for himself if he will listen to or produce musical "apples" or "onions." This decision is not an easy one. However, our decisions concerning our entertainment can influence us for the rest of our lives. As the poet Robert Frost wrote, "Two roads diverged in a wood, and I—/I took the one less traveled by,/ And that has made all the difference."[13]

References

Chapter 1. A Spiritual Approach to a Sensitive Subject

Chapter opening quote: As quoted in Boyd K. Packer, "Inspiring Music—Worthy Thoughts," *Ensign* 4 (January 1974): 28.

1. James E. Faust, "Trying to Serve the Lord Without Offending the Devil" (Brigham Young University devotional, 15 November 1994), typescript, pp. 1, 2.

2. *Man's Search for Happiness* (Salt Lake City: The Church of Jesus Christ of Latter-day Saints, 1964), videocassette.

3. Spencer W. Kimball, in Sydney Australia Area Conference Report, February 1976, pp. 54–55, emphasis in original.

4. *For the Strength of Youth* (Salt Lake City: The Church of Jesus Christ of Latter-day Saints, 1990), pp. 11, 13–14.

Chapter 2. Music and Our Lives

Chapter opening quote: Boyd K. Packer, "Personal Revelation: The Gift, the Test, and the Promise," *Ensign* 24 (November 1994): 61.

1. David O. McKay, "Music . . . the Universal Language," *Improvement Era* 62 (January 1959): 15.

2. As quoted in Boyd K. Packer, "Inspiring Music—Worthy Thoughts," *Ensign* 4 (January 1974): 25.

3. Stewart Powell et al., "What Entertainers Are Doing to Your Kids," *Newsweek,* 28 October 1985, p. 46.

4. Ibid.

5. Spencer W. Kimball, "Absolute Truth," *Ensign* 8 (September 1978): 3–4.

6. Gene R. Cook, *13 Lines of Defense* (Salt Lake City: Deseret Book Co., 1991), audiocassette.

7. As quoted in Jim Miller et al., "Is Rock on the Rocks?" *Newsweek,* 19 April 1982, p. 104.

8. Heber J. Grant, "Songs of the Heart," *Improvement Era* 43 (September 1940): 522.

9. As quoted in Packer, "Inspiring Music," p. 28.

Chapter 3. "For My Soul Delighteth in the Song of the Heart"

Chapter opening quote: Boyd K. Packer, "Inspiring Music—Worthy Thoughts," *Ensign* 4 (January 1974): 25.

1. As quoted in Doug Bassett, *Kisses at the Window* (Salt Lake City: Hawkes Publishing, 1985), pp. 75–76.

2. Joseph F. Smith, *Gospel Doctrine,* 14th ed. (Salt Lake City: Deseret Book Co., 1939), pp. 435–36.

3. Boyd K. Packer, "Reverence Invites Revelation," *Ensign* 21 (November 1991): 22.

4. Bruce R. McConkie, *The Promised Messiah* (Salt Lake City: Deseret Book Co., 1978), p. 553.

5. David O. McKay, "Music . . . the Universal Language," *Improvement Era* 62 (January 1959): 15.

6. Ibid.

7. Heber J. Grant, "Songs of the Heart," *Improvement Era* 43 (September 1940): 522.

8. John Taylor, *The Gospel Kingdom,* sel. G. Homer Durham (Salt Lake City: Bookcraft, 1943), p. 62.

9. As quoted in "Music 'Gracious Praise of God,'" *Church News,* 28 August 1983, p. 2.

10. Preface, *Hymns,* 1985, p. ix.

11. Dallin H. Oaks, "Worship Through Music," *Ensign* 24 (November 1994): 10, 12.

12. George Albert Smith, "The Power and Importance of Sincere Singing," *Improvement Era* 54 (March 1951): 141–42.

13. Packer, "Inspiring Music," p. 10.

14. Boyd K. Packer, "The Arts and the Spirit of the Lord," in *1976 Devotional Speeches of the Year* (Provo, Utah: Brigham Young University Press, 1977), p. 268.

15. Boyd K. Packer, "Personal Revelation: The Gift, the Test, and the Promise," *Ensign* 24 (November 1994): 61.

Chapter 4. Opposition in All Things

Chapter opening quote: Joseph Smith, *Teachings of the Prophet Joseph Smith,* sel. Joseph Fielding Smith (Salt Lake City: Deseret Book Co., 1976), p. 162.

1. Bruce R. McConkie, *The Promised Messiah* (Salt Lake City: Deseret Book Co., 1978), p. 553.

2. Bernard P. Brockbank, in Glasgow Scotland Area Conference Report, June 1976, p. 14.

3. As quoted in Boyd K. Packer, "Inspiring Music—Worthy Thoughts," *Ensign* 4 (January 1974): 25.

4. David B. Haight, "The Responsibility of Young Aaronic Priesthood Bearers," *Ensign* 11 (May 1981): 41.

5. Spencer W. Kimball, *The Miracle of Forgiveness* (Salt Lake City: Bookcraft, 1969), p. 175.

6. LeGrand Richards, "Call of the Prophets," *Ensign* 11 (May 1981): 31–33.

7. As quoted in Kimball, *The Miracle of Forgiveness,* p. 232.

8. David O. McKay, "Christ, the Light of Humanity," *Improvement Era* 71 (June 1968): 5.

9. Robert L. Backman, Vaughn J Featherstone, and Rex D. Pinegar, in "Letters to the Youth of the Church," *Church News,* 9 May 1981, p. 91.

Chapter 5. Making the Music Decision

1. Ezra Taft Benson, "To the Young Women of the Church," *Ensign* 16 (November 1986): 84.

2. Gordon B. Hinckley, "Fear Not to Do Good," *Ensign* 13 (May 1983): 80.

3. In *How Do I Choose?* (Salt Lake City: The Church of Jesus Christ of Latter-day Saints, 1980), p. 8.

4. Larry Bastian, in "I Have a Question," *Ensign* 4 (July 1974): 14.

5. Spencer W. Kimball, *The Teachings of Spencer W. Kimball,* ed. Edward L. Kimball (Salt Lake City: Bookcraft, 1982), p. 394.

6. Boyd K. Packer, "Inspiring Music—Worthy Thoughts," *Ensign* 4 (January 1974): 25, 27.

7. H. Burke Peterson, "'Touch Not the Evil Gift, Nor the Unclean Thing,'" *Ensign* 23 (November 1993): 42–43, emphasis in original.

8. Joseph F. Smith, "A Sermon on Purity," *Improvement Era* 6 (May 1903): 503–4.

9. Dennis Kneale, "Advertisers Use Music Groups to Reach Young Consumers," *Wall Street Journal,* 28 July 1983.

10. Frank Spotnitz, "Music Videos' Influence Spreads," *Deseret News TV Week,* 10 March 1985, p. 17.

11. John Taylor, in *Journal of Discourses* 26:31.

12. Boyd K. Packer, *Let Not Your Heart Be Troubled* (Salt Lake City: Bookcraft, 1991), p. 50.

13. Boyd K. Packer, "Little Children," *Ensign* 16 (November 1986): 17, emphasis added.

14. Boyd K. Packer, "Personal Revelation," *Ensign* 24 (November 1994): 61.

15. Kimball, *The Teachings of Spencer W. Kimball,* p. 285.

16. *TV Show Biz Magazine,* 15–21 January 1984, p. 41.

17. "Children Having Children," *Time,* 9 December 1985, p. 81.

18. *Rockin' in the '80s,* pp. 94–95.

19. As quoted in Michael Medved, *Hollywood vs. America* (New York: Harper Perennial, 1992), p. 194.

20. Victor B. Cline, "Obscenity: How It Affects Us, How We Can Deal with It," *Ensign* 14 (April 1984): 33–34, emphasis in original.

21. Kimball, *The Teachings of Spencer W. Kimball*, p. 283.

22. As quoted in Gordon B. Hinckley, "Building Your Tabernacle," *Ensign* 22 (November 1992): 51.

23. Ibid., pp. 51–52.

Chapter 6. Music and Our Actions, Feelings, and Thoughts

1. As quoted in Ezra Taft Benson, "Satan's Thrust—Youth," *Ensign* 1 (December 1971): 53.

2. Ibid.

3. John Diamond, *Your Body Doesn't Lie* (New York: Warner Books, 1979), p. 155.

4. As quoted in Hal Williams, "Dr. Nibley on Acquiring a Taste for Classical Music," *BYU Today*, April 1980, p. 14.

5. *The Plain Truth*, September 1980, p. 14.

6. Williams, "Dr. Nibley," p. 14.

7. Diamond, *Your Body Doesn't Lie*, p. 165.

8. Ibid., pp. 160–63.

9. Ibid., p. 164.

10. Ibid.

11. Bill Hendrick, "Filling Brains with Music May Help Kids Develop Learning Skills," *Deseret News*, 4 August 1994.

12. *Family Weekly*, 4 October 1970, p. 14.

13. Georgie Losinov, *Super Learning* (New York: Dell Publishing, 1979), pp. 62–76.

14. John E. Gibson, "You and the Invisible Power of Music," *Family Weekly*, 22 February 1976, p. 11.

15. Janice Johnson, "Making Life in the Womb More Interesting," *USA Weekend*, 8–10 November 1985, p. 31.

16. *Family Weekly*, 4 October 1970, p. 14.

17. As quoted in Bob Oliphant, "Music and Its Effects," type-script, p. 15.

18. Napoleon Hill, *Think and Grow Rich* (New York: Fawcett Crest, 1970), p. 28.

19. Denis Waitley, *The Psychology of Winning* (New York: Berkley Books, 1984), p. 95.

20. *Family Weekly,* 4 October 1970, p. 14.

21. Gibson, "You and the Invisible Power," p. 11.

22. As quoted in Thomas S. Monson, "The Path to Peace," *Ensign* 24 (May 1994): 61.

23. Spencer W. Kimball, *The Teachings of Spencer W. Kimball,* ed. Edward L. Kimball (Salt Lake City: Bookcraft, 1982), p. 519.

24. Boyd K. Packer, "Inspiring Music—Worthy Thoughts," *Ensign* 4 (January 1974): 27–28, emphasis in original.

25. Ibid, p. 28, emphasis in original.

26. "Bowl Over a Pig: Croon for Your Cow," *Family Weekly,* 27 January 1985, p. 18.

27. Barbara Bernstein, "Lizards Like Symphony but Hide from Rock," *Ogden Standard Examiner,* April 1981.

28. Williams, "Dr. Nibley," p. 15.

Chapter 7. Listening to a Prophet's Voice

Chapter opening quote: Ezra Taft Benson, "To the 'Youth of the Noble Birthright,'" *Ensign* 16 (May 1986): 43.

1. Scott Iwasaki, "Nails Leader Upset over Ban of Band," *Deseret News,* 20 October 1994.

2. Joseph Smith, *Teachings of the Prophet Joseph Smith,* comp. Joseph Fielding Smith (Salt Lake City: Deseret Book Co., 1976), p. 194.

3. Charles H. Gabriel, "I Stand All Amazed," *Hymns,* 1985, no. 193.

4. Heber J. Grant, *Gospel Standards,* sel. G. Homer Durham (Salt Lake City: Bookcraft, 1941), p. 170.

5. As quoted in Boyd K. Packer, "Inspiring Music—Worthy Thoughts," *Ensign* 4 (January 1974): 25.

6. Ezra Taft Benson, *The Teachings of Ezra Taft Benson* (Salt Lake City: Bookcraft, 1988), p. 326.

7. Neal A. Maxwell, "The Old Testament: Relevancy Within Antiquity," *The Third Annual Church Educational System Religious Educators' Symposium* (Salt Lake City: The Church of Jesus Christ of Latter-day Saints, 1979), p. 12.

8. Packer, "Inspiring Music," p. 27.

9. Ezra Taft Benson, "To the Youth of the Church," *Ensign* 16 (November 1986): 84.

10. Neal A. Maxwell, *Even As I Am* (Salt Lake City: Deseret Book Co., 1982), p. 104.

11. As quoted in Lynne Hollstein, "President Kimball Addresses 18,000 at U," *Church News,* 3 March 1979, p. 3.

12. As quoted in Frank C. Davis, "1,000th Stake Is Created," *Church News,* 24 February 1979, pp. 9–10.

Chapter 8. Never Fearing Truth

1. Joseph B. Wirthlin, "Live in Obedience," *Ensign* 24 (May 1994): 40.

For Parents and Youth Leaders: A Solution

Chapter opening quote: Sidney Lanier, as quoted in H. L. Mencken, ed., *A New Dictionary of Quotations* (New York: Alfred A. Knopf, 1942), p. 827.

1. As quoted in Marion D. Hanks, "Just One Boy," *Improvement Era* 62 (December 1959): 927.

2. Steve Huntley and Harold R. Kennedy, "Expert Advice: Keep Control of Family Fun," *U.S. News and World Report,* 28 October 1985, p. 54.

3. Ibid.

4. Ibid.

5. "A Conversation with Bruno Bettelheim: TV Stereotypes 'Devastating' to Young Minds," *U.S. News and World Report,* 28 October 1985, p. 55.

6. Ezra Taft Benson, in Philippine Islands Area Conference Report, August 1975, p. 10.

7. Heber J. Grant, in Conference Report, April 1934, p. 105.

8. As quoted in Boyd K. Packer, "The Arts and the Spirit of the Lord," in *1976 Devotional Speeches of the Year* (Provo, Utah: Brigham Young University Press, 1977), p. 268.

9. Ibid., pp. 273–74.

10. Ibid., p. 277.

11. Joseph Fielding Smith, *Take Heed to Yourselves!* 2nd ed. (Salt Lake City: Deseret Book Co., 1971), p. 36.

12. *Man's Search for Happiness* (Salt Lake City: The Church of Jesus Christ of Latter-day Saints, 1964), videocassette.

13. Robert Frost, "The Road Not Taken," *The Poetry of Robert Frost* (New York: Henry Holt and Co., 1979), p. 105.

Index